T0381504

WAR STORY

Swordfish Able Leader

BY CAPTAIN RAY M. BROWN

By Captain Ray M. Brown.
First Edition
Copyright August 31, 2001,
By
United States Copyright Office

Order this book online at www.trafford.com
or email orders@trafford.com

Most Trafford titles are also available at major online book retailers.

Print information available on the last page.

ISBN: 978-1-4120-8628-8 (sc)

Because of the dynamic nature of the Internet, any web addresses or links contained in this book may have changed
since publication and may no longer be valid. The views expressed in this work are solely those of the author and do
not necessarily reflect the views of the publisher, and the publisher hereby disclaims any responsibility for them.

Any people depicted in stock imagery provided by Getty Images are models, and
such images are being used for illustrative purposes only.
Certain stock imagery © Getty Images.

Trafford rev. 08/16/2019

Trafford
PUBLISHING® www.trafford.com
North America & international
toll-free: 844-688-6899 (USA & Canada)
fax: 812 355 4082

Licensed Illustrations used with Permission of Boeing Corporation

CAPTAIN RAY M. BROWN, 1943

Dedicated To

The fine Command Lead Aircrew members
who lost their life in air combat.
God Bless You for your heroic, ultimate sacrifice.

Captain Ray M. Brown

Acknowledgments

91st Bomb Group	*Research Data*
http://www.91stbombgroup.com	
Jack Gaffney	*401st Bomb Squadron Research*
91st BGMA	*Research Data*
World II Veterans	*Comments*
Mary Shaull	*Photograph*
Boeing Company	*Photographs*
Immanuel J Klette	*Col(Ret) Advisor*

Preface

My name is Paula Brown. I am a daughter of Ray Brown, the author of *Swordfish-Able-Leader.*

I recently uncovered a narrative written 60 years ago by my father about his World War II air combat experiences in the 8th Air Force.

I knew my father was a veteran but we never discussed World War II beyond the point that he was a Pilot in the European Theatre of Operation (ETO). Upon Separation from the Air Force, while recovering from surgery, my father wrote this narrative. It was for the family alone—it was never shared.

It is a tantalizing story of air combat service from start to finish. It offers specific information, dates and events, and explanations of factual historical interest. This narrative exhibits how U.S. Airmen bet their lives to get the job done, defending right from wrong. Patriotism is exhibited throughout the narrative. It exhibits the commitments of World War II veterans to liberate war victims at all costs. There is a spiritual commitment that these young American men must have felt. You don't have to read between the lines to recognize loyalty - it's all there.

I feel strongly that the heroic efforts of these young American veteran airmen should be aired for public view.

My father finally agreed to share his remarkable experience and *Swordfish-Able-Leader* was born. My father is a modest private man who belonged to the young generation of that time. He was conspicuously silent about his war experiences and achievements as were many combat veterans. His *tour of combat duty* saga contains specific life and death events and air combat struggles, which in come cases, are horrifying.

After reading this narrative it was clearer to me than ever before that World War II was a great catastrophe with the loss of life of the best young men that the country could provide. It impacted every household. The country suffered from it as well. This narrative piqued my interest in World War II. My father's medals have a brighter shine now that they are displayed and a greater luster as I contemplate how they were earned.

I studied the citations of a number of World War II air combat heroes and decided to write my own citation in honor of my father's performance. The citation specifically refers to a horrifying low-level bombing mission on the Merseburg refinery complex in November 1944. He was the *Lead* Pilot on this mission and survived devastating losses of B-17's and aircrews.

I regret to add that he is the sole survivor of his Lead aircrew – eight of the ten crew members died in air combat.

Citation

BROWN, RAY M. JR.

Rank and Organization: Captain, USAF, 1st Division, 1st Combat Wing, 9th Bomb Group, 324th Bomb Squadron, 8th Air Force.

Place and Date: Merseburg, Germany, Refinery and Oil Complex, November 21, 1944. Entered service at Santa Ana, California as air cadet.

Born: September 19, 1918; Fresno California

Go No.: _____No: _____ Date: _____

Citation: For Conspicuous gallantry and intrepidity above and beyond the call of duty in action with the enemy on 21 November 1944. On this date, he led a relatively small group of B-17 (H) Heavy Bombers successfully on a daring low-level visual bombing attack against the heavily defended Merseburg, Germany Refinery and Oil Complex. In late 1944, Allied Commands in the European Theater of Operation found it essential to immobilize the increasingly successful German motorized attacks on Allied invasion forces. The flow of oil, grease, and fuel from the Merseburg Refinery and Oil Complex to these German motorized units had to cease. Previous bombing missions had been only marginally successful. Bomber attack, even at high altitude, had suffered large loss of A/C and aircrews.

On 21 November 1944, Captain Brown and his command crew led the 8th Air Force on the important bombing mission to destroy Merseburg. Flying and bombing conditions at the briefed 27000' bombing altitude found this important target obscured. A low-level visual bombing attack risked complete annihilation of the attacking bombers and crews with few survivors. With full knowledge of personal risks and the implications of devastating losses, Captain Brown and his command crew directed and led a visual low-level attack on the highly defended Merseburg, Germany Refinery and Oil Complex. Most of the 8th Air Force aborted the hazardous mission due to the poor bombing conditions and bombed alternate and less-defended targets of opportunity. Although successful, only a fraction of those B-17's and aircrews attacking Merseburg survived. Returning B-17's suffered predictable heavy battle damage and high loss of aircrew. The decision for a visual low-level bombing attack was heroic considering risks of survival. Captain Brown's extraordinary expertise and skill in maneuvering the attack with a short visual bomb run and regrouping the damaged surviving damage B-17 aircraft under devastating anti-aircraft fire and fighter opposition was credited to saving many of the crippled surviving B-17's and aircrews. The actual witnessed damage was spectacular. Lt. General Doolittle, Commander of the 8th Air Force sent a special commendation—"For your outstanding efforts and personal bravery in carrying out the tasks assigned under grave and seemingly insurmountable difficulties." Later analysis indicated that this Merseburg mission, though costly in loss of A/C equipment as well as loss of life, contributed to a successful allied invasion and shortened World War II in Europe. By his extraordinary flying and air combat skills, gallant leadership and intrepidity; Captain Ray M. Brown rendered outstanding, distinguished, and valorous services to our nation.

USAF 91st Bomb Group

This Book would be incomplete without reflecting on the beginnings of the 91st Bomb Group and its place in air combat history in World War II.

The 8th Air Force was centered in England in 1942 with a responsibility to organize a major U.S. heavy bombardment action in the European Theater of Operations (ETO). The 8th Air Force ultimately commanded 350,000 men and women in its operations—this included 43 Heavy Bomb Groups, 4 Medium Bomb Groups, and 20 Fighter Groups. The Heavy Bomb Groups were organized into three Divisions and flew B-17's and B-24's.

The 8th Air Force flew 330,523 bomb sorties, during which 26,000, airmen were killed, 7000 wounded, and 28,000 survived as prisoners of war. Over 686,406 tons of explosive bombs were delivered and 15,731 enemy aircraft were destroyed.

The 91st Bomb Group (H) was nicknamed the "Ragged Irregulars", since heavy losses and battle damage often prevented them from organizing a full 54 B-17 Group formation. The 91st (H) Bomb Group flew its first mission on 7 November, 1942 when it supplied 14 B-17F's to the first USAF 54 B-17F operational mission. In 1945, the 91st Bomb Group (H) supplied 54 B-17G's to a 1200 B-17G USAF operational mission.

The 91st Bomb Group (H) was based at Bassingbourn, England in the 1st Division, 1st Combat Wing. It was organized with 4 Bomb Squadrons: the 322nd, the 323rd, the 324th, and the 401st.

It distinguished itself in air combat operations from 7 November, 1942 to 25 April, 1945. The 91st Bomb Group (H) flew 340 missions, dropping 22,142 tons of explosive bombs. Over 400 B-17F's and B-17G's were utilized during the ETO operations. 197 B-17F's and B-17G's were lost in action, and 1010 airmen were killed or missing in action.

The 91st Bomb Group (H) flew the most bombing missions of any Bomb Group in the U.S. 8th Air Force with the highest losses of airmen and aircraft. It was commended for leading the total Air Force on several missions where the targets were critical to the war and the enemy defenses were almost unsurmountable:

17 August, 1943———-Schweinfurt, Germany(Losses 43%)

21st November, 1944—Merseburg Oil Complex(Losses 35%)

This Book relates to the Merseburg Oil Complex mission, since the Author was the Lead Command Pilot of the Merseburg mission.

War

A few comments about the word, "War", which has new contemporary significance in post "nine-eleven" thinking. It is difficult to define the concept of war. The important thoughts that matter may differ in each person's mind. Often the concept is deeply biased by a single action or event.

The question of fabricating a definition of War posed itself during the writing of this narrative over 60 years ago, and now it is in its recent editing. In my view, War is a compendium of events, thoughts, ideals and facts that project a true mental picture of the conflict.

For example:Enter an artist's gallery with scores of paintings displayed on the walls. As you sight each painting you draw a conclusion. The conclusion may be pleasant or unpleasant – beautiful or ugly – mind boggling or rational – or even meaningless. Nevertheless, it is the kaleidoscope of impressions in their totality that describe the experience.

This narrative was divided into a multiplicity of chapters that vary in content to provide this total experience, much like viewing the paintings. It was important to add facts and feelings to explore the broad experience of war actions in their most informative, yet grim aspects.

Table of Contents

Foreword

The present interest in locating and completing the World War II Memorial in Washington D.C. and the sad fact that World War II veterans are dying rapidly are vivid reminders of war and consequence.

The heinous terrorist acts in New York City and Washington D.C. on September 11, 2001 caused a horror and anguish that changed our lives significantly. We are at War and the consequences will be dramatic!

This Terrorist War differs from prior wars in that it violated soil, property, and lives of the American people at Home. While the conduct of this Terrorist War may be different from other wars in manner, involvement, and strategy, it nonetheless triggers an emerging rebirth of the same inspiring American patriotism experienced in World War II. The Flag is important and it must wave majestically forever!

It is worth noting that the heroic efforts of all Americans involved in the rescue efforts in the aftermath of the terrorist acts exhibit the same patterns of courage as those of young American aircrews discussed in this World War II narrative.

My personal experience in (H) Heavy Bomber air combat in the European Theater of Operation (ETO) began in 1944. I completed 30 combat missions and 230 combat flying hours in B-17 (H) Heavy Bombers with the USAF 1st Division; 1st Combat Wing; 91st

Bomb Group and 324th Bomb Squadron at Bassingbourn, England. I regret to say that I am the sole survivor of my Lead aircrew - eight of the ten crew members died in air combat.

It is my hope and avid desire to provide an interesting dialogue of (H) Heavy Bomber air combat experience in a WWII war period from start to finish. Perhaps some readers might relive this experience while families of ETO WWII aircrews might recall some of the events and circumstances that impacted their own lives. Others might be interested in the details and facts of air combat that made history over 60 years ago.

Veterans of World War II have been conspicuously silent about events and circumstances of their personal war experiences. The narrative that follows was written over 60 years ago as a private and detailed report for my family alone. With patriotism in World Wars reviving, my family has chosen to share these memoirs with others.

"B-17G In Flight"

Timeline

World War II events need to be placed in a point in time to understand the implications of "Swordfish Able Leader" and the tour of duty that it describes.

World War II began with the German Nazi's invasion of Poland on September 1st, 1939.

World War II for America started with the surprise Japanese bombing and destruction of American Pacific sea power anchored in Pearl Harbor and the adjoining military Bases, Clarke and Hickam Fields on December 7th 1941. It was a monstrous military event that galvanized America to declare War on Japan on December 8th 1941. This was the beginning of America's involvement in World War II., although Germany with its Nazi movement was active in war actions in Europe.

World War II expanded to Africa on November 8, 1942, a year after Pearl Harbor, and the Pacific action expanded to Guadalcanal and other adjoining islands occupied by Japanese. The Allied invasion of Africa on November 8, 1942 initiated actions that ultimately resulted in the invasion of southern Europe through Italy.

Great Britain collaborated with America in 1942 to organize a land and sea invasion force and an Air Force to support land troops and neutralize the highly developed German industrial complexes that serviced the German military machine.

The Royal Air Force (RAF) was dedicated to short-distance night bombing—USAF, to daylight deep penetration day bombing. Together, the RAF and USAF complemented each other to maintain constant pressure on Germany.

The 8th Air Force was created on January 28th 1942. England was the center of Allied activity for the invasion of Europe. English air bases were converted to American standards for B-17 and B-24 heavy bomber operations in mid 1942 and early 1943. American fighter bases were also constructed. The first 8th Air Force organized bombing mission was August, 1942.

The first B-17 and B-24 "maximum effort" occurred on August 17th 1943 —the prime target, a critical ball-bearing factory in Schweinfurt, Germany. Final demolition of the Schweinfurt, Germany ball-bearing factory was accomplished on October 14, 1943. At this time the total Air Force heavy bombers were less than 300. The B-17 and B-24 aircrew losses at Schweinfurt, Germany were enormous—losses exceeded 100, or more, aircraft and 1,000 air men with heavy battle damage.

The Royal Air Force (RAF) had planned to operate B-17's and B-24's, but declined to utilize the aircraft due to their perception of its slow speed and vulnerability. America, however, continued to operate both aircraft throughout World War II in spite of high losses of both aircraft and aircrew.

Preparations for invasion of France continued until the Normandy invasion occurred on June 6, 1944. After the debacle at Schweinfurt, Germany, the USAF refurbished their B-17F inventory and aircrews. Selected bombing missions with limited exposure to the Luftwaffe were resumed in late 1943 and into early 1944, but high loss rates continued. The November, 1944 destruction of Merseburg Oil and Refinery Complex by USAF 8th AF B-17G aircraft was a major and final blow to the German Western Armies—their mechanized units ran out of fuel.

American fighter support with long-range capabilities were needed. "Ram-rod" P-51's and P-47's, modified with disposable wing "drop" tanks, were added to the inventory of fighter aircraft in December, 1943. The B-17G resulted from modifications to the B-17F in

July, 1943. The modifications included more armor, a "chin" turret for frontal fighter attacks, and other changes to improve defense against the German Luftwaffe. These modifications were urgently needed to resume dangerous deep penetrations into industrial Germany and to defend again the German Luftwaffe.

The B-17G entered the active inventory in early 1944, and the long range penetrations to German industrial complexes were resumed. The B-17G inventory was implemented by new aircrews flying B-17G aircraft across the North Atlantic in early to mid-1944. By D-Day, the USAF bomber inventory approached 1,000 heavy B-17 and B-24 modified heavy bombers, and the strategic deep penetrations were resumed.

By late 1944, the Luftwaffe fighter attacks had diminished in effectiveness, since fuel, aircraft production, replacement parts, and experienced pilots to fly the German F-109's and FW-190's were not available.

The famous "Battle of the Bulge" started on December 16, 1944. This was followed by the union (meeting) of the Soviet troops and the American troops in Germany on April 25th 1945.

Germany surrendered on VE Day, May 7, 1945 ending the European phase of World War II.

The Japanese were adamant about surrender to the Allies under any circumstances, preferring death to defeat. An Atomic bomb was dropped on Hiroshima, Japan on August 6th, 1945, followed by a second atomic bomb on Nagasaki, Japan on August 9th 1945. As a result of this cataclysmic occurrence, Japan surrendered on August 15th, 1945. This finalized the World War II combat conflict.

The saga of "Swordfish Able Leader" was active in the ETO from late May, 1944 until Christmas Day, December 25, 1944.

In The Beginning

As so many young Americans, I watched the beautiful, somewhat exotic P-38 twin-boomed fighters scream across the sky and the imposing 4-engine B-17 (H) Heavy Bombers fly by majestically. The beautiful *silver wings* worn by the pilots who flew these machines were a thing of glory and dreams.

I took my qualification examinations in the Army Air Corp in Portland Oregon where I was a successful Manager of the Northwest Region for the Ethyl Corporation. I requested a Military Leave of Absence, and entered the Army Air Force at Santa Ana, California in December 1942 as Private Ray M. Brown (19102911). Later, I was granted entry to the Army Air Force cadet system.

Primary pilot training was at Rankin Academy in Tulare, California, where after four hours of flight instruction, I successfully soloed in a Stearman bi-wing trainer.

Basic training was at the Royal Air Force (RAF) Station at Lancaster, California, where experience in BT-13 basic single engine trainers occurred.

Advanced training in twin –engine advanced aircraft was at Marfa, Texas. When the advanced multi-engine training was completed, I was awarded Second Lieutenant Officer credentials and my coveted *silver wings*.

When awarding my silver wings, a Colonel reminded us, "Look to your left, gentlemen, and then to your right. The man to your left will die in air combat." While feeling sorry for the pilot on one's left, I also realized great epiphany that to my right was another pilot who saw me at his left. As you will note later, the Colonel was close to fact. In my class, both the pilots to my left and right were combat casualties. Most were assigned to the European Theater of Operation (ETO) in (H) Heavy Bombardment. Of my graduating group of 35 pilots assigned to air combat, only 5 survived the first 20 missions. Today, as far as I know, I am the lone survivor of my graduating class. I am also the last survivor of my European theater of Operations (ETO) Lead Command Aircrew, which perished in air combat.

Before reaching the ETO, I was assigned to Roswell, New Mexico AAFB where I received advanced training as a First Pilot in B-17F's. Upon successful completion of the arduous training at Roswell AAFB, I was then sent to Salt Lake City, Utah for aircrew assignment.

Not Ten Men – A Combat Crew (B-17)

We were a collection of young men from average American homes, from practically every corner of the United States. This is a story of just ten of these average persons, who individually may have been a clerk in Paducah, a butcher in Pomona, or an engineer in Detroit; just plain young Mr. Americans. But together we made up one of those bomber crews that flew air combat in the ETO.

There were ten of us: four Second Lieutenants and six Enlisted Men. We were assembled to hear our names associated together for the first time at a staging area in Salt Lake City, Utah. It was cold that 27th of February 1944, as we stood in snow to our ankles in a freezing wind. After all our individual training, we were in the process of being born a combat crew that memorable February morning.

"Pilots will be called on roll-call. Crews line up behind your pilot," announced the Officer in charge. At last, Crew No. FO-CJ-77 (3475) came into being:

Pilot	Brown, R.M. Jr.	Fullerton, CA
Co-pilot	Carbery, J.S.	Long Island, NY
Navigator	Boyd, R.T.	Detroit, MI
Bombardier	Guzek, L.A.	Chicago, IL
Engineer	Gunner Rader, M.H.	

Radio Operator	Braam, N.C. Jr.	Chicago, IL
Armorer-Waist Gunner	MacDonald, R.R.	
Ball-Turret Gunner	McDonough, J.V.	
Waist Gunner	McHolland, A.B.	
Tail Gunner	Gilbertson, R.A.	

Our first meeting was brief. The Officers and Enlisted Men were separated to board a troop train, better described as a human cattle car that served its purpose poorly.

Our first destination was Dyersburg AAFB, Tennessee. We arrived dirty and grouchy. Our Officers' *Pinks* (cream-colored dress trousers) closely resembled the tattletale gray color of camping breeches. As we disembarked the troop train, we could be described in military terms as just plain *raunchy*.

We marched to the mess hall, and drew quarters. Our Officers' quarters were actually tents with boards instead of canvas, but they were reasonably comfortable. A problem was that it was more than a mile to the flight line through good old slippery Tennessee mud.

Our crew training started with lectures, ground school, conferences, link trainer, bomb trainer, responsibilities, and gunnery. After a week of expectancy and a full diet of preparatory work, I had a general idea that a first pilot not only flew the airplane but understood each crewmember's job, in addition to doubling as a leader, coordinator, Father Confessor, and broadly speaking, a "papa" to the aircrew.

For three months I cajoled, pampered, learned, studied, and in Army idiom *"chewed"* and in turn was *"chewed."* But for it all, we graduated a well-knit crew, an integral unit, trained in simulated combat conditions, yet untried. We had our incidents, yet our crew was the better for it all.

For instance, we had a malfunction in our B-17E bomb-bay doors. One of our bomb-bay doors snapped loose, while the other bomb-bay door froze open. The free-swinging bomb-bay door ripped the whole underside of the B-17E. An emergency landing had to be made with bomb-bay doors open, one hanging loose and swinging free in a 25 mph cross wind. Crew discipline was excellent, and I landed the B-17 safely.

Another incident was the loss of an engine on take-off. Still another, was an engine fire. Another, was a cockpit electrical fire, but again in each case, the crew worked together as a team. We came through with an excellent record - and all of us were alive and proud.

We were finished with the preliminaries. Next came the real thing - combat. We were a cocky lot, but we sobered later as we experienced the realities of air combat.

Orders came through for Crew 3475. Our destination was Kearney AAFB, Nebraska. Another troop-train ride, more grime, card games, and waiting, but this time our spirits were high with anticipation!

We were processed again when we disembarked at Kearney AAFB. New flying clothes were issued and physical examinations were ordered. We tested our new B-17G flown directly from the modification factory, and believe it, it's true, we were subjected to more ground school.

The B-17 and B-24 Four-Engine Heavy Bombers

The B-17F "Flying Fortress" was the first model of a Boeing four-engine heavy bomber to see service in World War II. After several months of air combat, the B-17F was faulted for inadequate protection from German Luftwaffe fighter frontal attacks. The Luftwaffe ME-109 and FW190 fighters focused on frontal attacks to destroy the leading command aircraft in the formation causing major confusion in the bomber formation. The B-17 was generally noted for its rugged construction and was the main heavy bomber used in the European Theater of Operations (ETO). The B-24 "Liberator" was also an active combat aircraft used in the ETO.

USAF First Division and Third Division featured B-17's—The Second Division featured B-24's.

In early 1944, the B-17G, a modified B-17F, was introduced with a "chin" 50 caliber machine gun turret to protect against formation frontal attacks. The modification was effective and the German Luftwaffe changed their combat strategy to side attacks and rear attacks. There were other modifications to armor and controls in the B-17G, and the B-17G bomber was effective for the remainder of World War II.

"B-17G's In Production"

The B-17G had a ceiling of 35,000 ft and a top speed at altitude of 310 mph. It had a range of 2000 miles with full fuel load and could carry 15,000 pounds of bombs. Over 12,700 B-17's of all models were produced.

The B-17G was heavily armored, outfitted with 50 caliber tail guns, two 50 caliber waist guns, two "greenhouse" 50 caliber guns, a "chin turret", an under-fuselage "ball" turret, and a pilot-cabin turret manned by the flight engineer. The B-17G could fly with only two engines if the other two were damaged. The aluminum metal skin could sustain major damage from enemy fighters and anti-aircraft (flak) without losing flight control. The B-17G was further modified as it entered combat conditions by removing wing icing "boots" and adding armor plate in various critical areas. Radios were modified for short-range operation to diminish "clatter and confusion" and various transponders and beacons related to air operations were installed. The Lead Command Bomber was outfitted with the famous Norden Bomb Sight, and often other equipment, such as the "Mickey" radar and/or H2X when "blind-bombing" was ordered.

The B-24 Bomber was a four engine heavy bomber that also saw active service in the ETO. It featured a tricycle landing gear system and a special wing design to provide high performance. The B-24 had a top speed of 310 mph at altitude and a ceiling of 30,000 feet. It had a range of over 3000 miles and could carry 15000 pounds of bombs. Over 18,000 B-24's were built during the World War II period.

Young of Heart

When I reported to the Santa Ana, California, Army Base to become a United States Army Air Force Cadet, I noted the young ages of the Cadets. The roster included mostly unmarried, college-educated, physically-healthy, and well-adjusted young men with a multiplicity of backgrounds ranging from professional to unemployed. At 24, I was among the older Cadets. The estimated average age of our 43-J Class was 21-22, so my age difference was not significant and did not impact on my training or assignments.

Each of the 10 member aircrew in B-17's were trained for months and tested for excellence. Again, the youngness of the entire aircrew made the flying program special. The closeness of aircrews was an ever-present asset which contributed to the psychological survival of the group under the death and destruction of the times.

At sunrise, while flying a long ten (10) hour "maximum effort" (ME) mission to Munich, Germany, the beauty of glittering and scintillating sunlight reflected from the wings and fuselages of hundreds of B-17's in front of our 91st Bomb Group formation. The Alps were unfolding to our right—the target ahead. It was wondrous sight and exciting!I remember at the time wondering how many of those 43-J Santa Ana Cadets that started with "wings" in their eyes were in this trailing formation of 1,200 B-17's. In this mission, it meant that over 12,000 of the best young men that America could offer were enroute to a deadly mission encounter with the enemy. Due to the deadly nature of this particular mission, probably over 1,000 of these airmen would not return to their Base this day. A few of the aircrews might parachute or crash land in Germany and escape death, but most would sacrifice their young life. This scenario was repeated over and over again for almost two years.

During my "tour of combat duty" of thirty (30) combat missions, there were very few aircrews that survived without losses. For example, I am the only survivor of my Lead Command Aircrew—eight of my ten-man aircrew died in air combat. The casualty rates of aircrews varied with the mission and the period that they were active in combat, but they were generally high and not discussed. The loss of these young airmen was a tragedy for America and the future of so many families.

The camaraderie among these young airmen was wondrous, and lifetime friendships were cemented in their lives as they proceeded with their "tour of combat duty". It often reflected itself in the hospitals when visiting those injured airmen that were fortunate enough to return to Base—laughter was a precious commodity when "you hurt so much!" So it was!

While loss of aircrews in a close-knit Squadron of 24 B-17's was treated seriously, the accounting of aircrew and B-17 losses were treated casually. The able squadron aircrew roster was kept on a large Squadron blackboard, listed under the first pilot's name and aircraft. When losses occurred, an eraser wiped out the listing—this was updated after every mission. There were times when erasures were overwhelming to our personal psyche, since these were not numbers but lists of our dear comrades. Replacement aircrews were flown in immediately, and missions of that Squadron were usually delayed a few days when casualties were high. The War had to continue, however, and the most recent erasures were filled with new names.

When not flying and the 91st Bomb Group "was out", the aircrews not on a mission and the ground crews gathered about the Bassingbourn (91st Bomb Group) Control Tower to listen to radio reports as the Group formation returned from a mission. As the first Squadron approached, the counting began. Soon the red-red flares indicating injured or dead began streaking over the runways—the flares indicated that these aircraft would be landing first for medical triage and transportation of the injured to the Base hospital. The other B-17's orbited the field once or twice before landing to accommodate treatment of their injured companions. Since there were few missions without aircraft losses and aircrew injuries, compassion flowed freely for those who were gone or injured.

The aftermath of a difficult combat mission was heart-breaking. As young men, the experience of mass loss of companions was sometimes a soul-wrenching experience that impacted their lives.

The ground crews with lost B-17's and aircrews sometimes wandered to their B-17 "hard-stand" (B-17 parking assignment) which was now vacant after the Group had landed. They looked forlorn as they sat on the turf about the "hard-stand". They often waited an hour or so, hoping by chance their aircrew was just delayed. This was not often the case. Before the day was out, a new B-17 with a replacement aircrew would occupy the space, and the War would continue.

Last of all, the finality of the tragedy of a lost crewman would be documented with a compassionate letter to the wife, mother, or family describing a friendship and the heroic contribution that had been made. Many veterans wrote these letters—it was a sad chore!

These heroic aircrews were magnificent when the whole of the world War 11 conflict is viewed. The youth that prevailed in "wheeling" B-17's loaded with deadly explosives over enemy targets is a saga of patriotism and dedication that Americans will hopefully never forget.

"B-17G LINE-UP"

<u>"B-17G In Flight"</u>

On Our Way

At 2300 hours, the 20th day of May 1944, we were briefed for the first leg of our flight to England. Our destination for the first leg of our flight was Grenier AAFB, New Hampshire. At 0030 hours the 21st day of May 1944, Crew 3475 left in a new B-17G, loaded to full gross weight of 64500 pounds. After flashing recognition to the tower's *green light* go-ahead signal, engines broke to full-powered roar, and we were OFF!

Weather was extreme with frontal activity over two-thirds of the briefed route. Icing, sleet, snow, and heavy rain made the first leg more task than pleasure. Three hundred miles from our destination, in heavy lightning and electrical disturbance, our radios were rendered inoperative, and navigation was difficult. We reached Grenier AAFB, New Hampshire, however, without further circumnavigation and trouble.

Repairs were made at Grenier AAFB where new equipment was issued and installed. After the delay, our Secret Orders were handed to us in a sealed container to be opened after leaving the continental limits of the United States. We left Grenier AAFB at 1030 hours in good weather on the 24th of May 1944. The Navigator, Lt. Boyd, called after several hours flight time, "Navigator to crew: you have just left the United States."

Secret Orders revealed that we were bound for Gander Field, Newfoundland, and then, as the third leg of our flight, 2200 miles over the North Atlantic Ocean to Valley, Wales.

Arrival at Gander Field, Newfoundland, was without difficulty with good weather all the distance. Rest, briefing, sandwiches, several days of delay for optimum weather, and at 1800 hours the 26th of May 1944, the same combat crew, Number 3475, took the green light for the last leg, *the big hop*— Gander, Newfoundland across the North Atlantic Ocean to Valley, Wales.

An interesting situation existed in North Atlantic B-17 transoceanic flights from Gander, Newfoundland to England in 1944. The transoceanic air mileage was at the extreme range of the B-17G (fully loaded). The B-17G specifications noted the maximum range (fully loaded) was 2,000 miles—the transoceanic flight was 2,200 miles. Three factors were necessary for a successful trip without *ditching* the aircraft in the North Atlantic. The first factor was that the prevailing winds along the course had to exceed an average of 25 knots in the direction of flight. The second factor was the need for accurate navigation, since extra mileage from errors could cause depletion of fuel before landfall. The third factor was selection of altitude with the most favorable directional winds and wind speed. Wind direction naturally changes as the flight progresses.

As the B-17G approached the coast of Ireland, a directional beacon called the Derrycross Beacon, provided a homing source for the Ireland landfall. The Germans were well aware of the problems of transoceanic flight of the B-17G's. Consequently, they appropriately located submarines south of the desired flight path. The German submarines then sent strong radio signals that mimicked the Derrycross Beacon, hoping to draw B-17G's off-course and to disaster. It was a clever German trick and successful in a few tragic cases. To show the effectiveness of the German trick, 30 B-17G's left Gander, Newfoundland singly on the date of our departure. It was reported upon our arrival that one B-17G, leaving before us, was lost at sea or landed elsewhere.

We left Newfoundland and headed over that vast expanse of the North Atlantic Ocean. A few icebergs were observed, then weather obscured all, since we climbed through and above a cloud layer to a specific briefed weather altitude to use wind to our advantage. Through the night and into the next day we cruised along, carefully computing gasoline consumption and changing headings to capture optimum wind speeds. As sunlight filtered through a break in the clouds, we caught sight of the coast of Ireland—a welcome and beautiful sight. We crossed the Irish Sea soon thereafter, and located Valley, Wales where the wheels touched and smoked down on the runway. A tired and happy crew parked one B-17G.

Waiting, Waiting, Waiting...
When Do We Fly

When we initiated our flight to England, it was our presumption that the B-17G we flew was to be ours, our combat craft. We were incorrect. Our flight was merely an accommodation for the Army Transport Command (ATC)—ferrying an aircraft to the European Theater of Operation (ETO). At our flight destination, Crew 3475 caught a last respectful glimpse of our first-owned *Flying Fortress*, which may, or may not have played an important role in the battle over Germany.

After closing the hatches of our B-17G for the last time, we began our processing and waiting. For two weeks the crew changed stations, separated, reformed, processed, and waited anxiously. From Valley, Wales, a seemingly miniature, almost a toy train delivered us to the 16th RCD, a general reception depot, which we called *Stone*. The train journey was a daylight trip, so our introduction to Britain's landscape was sightly. Our immediate impression, I recall, was that England is a picturesque country. Engrossed as we were in sightseeing, the trip was short.

At Stone our primary duty was one of anxious and expectant waiting for assignment to a Reception and Training Squadron, where our final combat assignments would be made.

All American money was exchanged at the current rate of exchange for English money. For us, as untraveled as we were, it was a seemingly baffling combination of pence, shillings, half crowns, pounds, guineas, and other denominations. The valuation, obscure and difficult at first, quickly adjusted itself in poker games. The food was wholesome, yet stripped of fanciness, and fundamentally designed for nourishment—nothing else.

On the 1st of June 1944, Crew 3475, Pilot Brown, R.M., was posted on orders for immediate departure. The Enlisted Men, with exception of the Radio Operator, were sent to a gunnery school on the east coast of England called *The Wash*. The four Officers and the Radio Operator were detoured to the 1st Replacement and Training Squadron, Bombardment, AAF Station 112. This station was commonly known as *Bovington*, which was the turning point for the German bombers during the blitz bombing of London.

More processing and waiting and training ensued which involved only ground instruction. Again our feet were firmly embedded in English mud for the time. We continued in our training lectures on aircraft identification, security measures, organization, procedures, technical developments, strategy, code, and navigational aids. A myriad of details filled our days, but no flying - not just yet.

One morning on the 6th of June 1944, as we sat in a sunrise class, a note of wonder and perhaps expectancy, or even anticipation invaded the room and permeated our thoughts. The bombers were out late this date and were flying low altitude—unusual, very unusual. Wave after wave of attack bombers, medium bombers, fighter-bombers, (H) Heavy Bombers, and fighters passed overhead. The aircraft appeared to be shuttling. All morning into the afternoon the air parade passed in review. Although no information was forthcoming immediately, we sensed the invasion of Western Europe had begun. Verification came through to us during late morning. Through fear of counter-measures, Bovington was alerted for gas attack. We carried gas masks and .45 cal. automatic Army pistol as a side-arm. Speculation and rumor ran rife. Two *red alerts* added fodder to the fire of speculation. Tension accentuated with knowledge that enemy intruder aircraft, or unidentified aircraft were in the proximity of Bovington. Our concerns increased due to secret aircraft experimental work that was being carried out at a presumably obscure airfield less than 1000 yards from our barracks. We faithfully turned out to the heavily barricaded and reinforced confines of our bomb shelters during alerts. Intelligence reports stressed the efficiency of German espionage, so our concerns were well founded.

Close interest centered about the TWX system—the military secret teletype system over which restricted, confidential, and secret information passed from one station to another. We learned the invasion was a success, with beachheads firmly established, and heavy bombing in progress. Our invasion tactics apparently had fooled the Germans, and the element of surprise had been reasonably successful.

The *Luftwaffe* was the name of the German Air Force. It was important to distract the German Luftwaffe from our landing effort for obvious reasons. Thousands of tons of radar material, metal strips similar to Christmas icicle decorations (we called it *chaff* or *window*) were used to confuse and disrupt German radar detection. Chaff created fictitious air armadas at a point far from the actual point of invasion. The German Luftwaffe scoured the sky for an air armada that was non-existent on this Day.

Landing and support craft of the Allied Nations, principally British, American, and Australian, set out from innumerable ports of embarkation and estuaries at night prior to the morning of June 6th, 1944. They sailed up the English Channel, ostensibly for a landing at a point considered the shortest distance from England to the Continent—pointed at Calais, France.

After setting course in the night, these craft backtracked and made the original landings on the Normandy Coast near the Cherbourg peninsula. Naval craft bombarded the German coast fortresses with high-powered naval guns, followed by bombs from medium and light bombers. The strategy was to neutralize the coast defenses. The results were considered and verified excellent.

An interesting sidelight was the fighter cover provided the huge landing operation. The landing originally was to be covered by all types of fighter aircraft. Last minute changes were instituted to allow only American P-38 fighter aircraft to provide close cover to the sea parade. This was due to the easily identifiable characteristics of the twin-boomed P-38 fighter plane.

It was assumed that under the possible poor visibility, that Navy and Army gunners might find it difficult to distinguish the American P-51 *Mustang* from the German Messerschmidt ME-109, as well as the American P-47 *Thunderbolt* from the German Folke Wulffe FW-190. Apparently it was a justifiable decision, for no difficulty expressed itself. On this day of invasion, every commissionable P-38 flew in close support of our ground and sea forces in transit. As the landing progressed, P-51's and P-47's entered the fray.

Our success distinguished itself by the efficiency and detail in which the plan unfolded and developed. There were gross errors, of course, but the first knockout blow in continental Western Europe had landed, and the enemy had momentarily been stunned. Progress at this time was assured, but the speed was the questionable unknown quantity. At first we were exhilarated, but slowly we realized we were dealt out of the *Big Game*. We were still to participate in the Big Game, but disappointment in not participating initially on *D-Day* was paramount.

All was not lost, however, since I received a happenstance pilot assignment for a brief reconnaissance flight late in the day to allow VIP witnesses to view the overall conditions at the French landing sites. Our initial navigation point was St. Lo, France. It was an awesome sight at sunset to witness the bloody-red beach water, the wreckage, and the general debris. It was clear that the landing was secure, but with a costly toll.

91ST BOMB GROUP PATCH

Assignment At Last

On the 15th of June 1944, our assignments to a Combat Bomb Group were posted. Our destination was the 91st Bombardment Group, (H) Heavy, APO 557, somewhere in England. Immediate facilities for departure were provided, and within six hours we had arrived at our new home. It was one of the more distinguished airfields in England, home of such famous *Flying Fortresses* as the *Memphis Belle*. Leased from the Royal Air Force (RAF), it had formerly been utilized as a field for RAF training, much as Kelly or Randolph AAF in San Antonio, Texas were used for U.S. pilots. Located near Royston, England, scarcely more than 12 miles southwest of Cambridge, the Air Base was called *Bassingborn*. We were thrilled, for at last we had arrived. Not only that, but we were assigned to a famous Air Base, a Base with accommodations, permanent quarters, permanent hangers, permanent mess halls, clubs, and even, mind you, hot water facilities.

Psyche

It is fascinating to reflect on the mindset of the aircrews as experience in combat molded new anxieties and mental attitudes.

As aircrews entered active combat squadrons, anxiousness to get into combat was overwhelming. The novice aircrews exuded confidence in their flying skills. In fact, the new untried aircrews resented practice sessions and other flight training such as close formation flying. Veterans were unusually thoughtful in their firm, but positive leadership during combat instructions and practice. The veterans had been there before! However, it was hard to temper the confidence of the novice aircrews prior to their first mission.

The impact of their first venture into air combat was overwhelming. The realization that combat was not an exercise, but a lethal game of life and death was implanted in their minds forever. To witness B-17 explosions, B-17 wings blown off, engine fires, as well as blood and guts and death was devastating. Again, the veterans were always role models for this *coming of combat* age. The anxiousness to fly the next mission was always more subdued as the novice aircrews started to think about "what could happen." The first mission usually tested the novice combat pilots in their flying skills. Flying in combat was different—very different. They understood practice flying and gunnery sessions better. Surviving the first several missions was always nerve-racking because casualties of novices were extremely high.

After ten missions, or so, it was difficult to become overconfident. The toll of combat experiences on the psyche made the nights long, sleep restless, and underlying fears of the future more prominent. Mind you, these were now evolving veterans—survivors to date! Again, the metamorphism of the psyche was firmly in place—establishing a mind-set.

After twenty or so missions, combat experience indelibly cemented the mind with sad and calamitous memories. These thoughts further impacted the psyche. While fear became more prominent, it had to be put aside.

As the tour of duty of 30 missions neared completion, the stress and strain became enormous. By this time, **survival** was the operative word.

In all these stages of gaining combat experience, it seemed inwardly that *veteran* was merely a word and not a state of mind.

No doubt about it, the psyche went through a painful process adapting to combat.

324ᵀᴴ BOMB SQUADRON PATCH

"THUMBS UP IN FLIGHT"

Combat At Last

After two years of training and planning and probably the most difficult of all, waiting, we were ready and willing, almost anxious to get started. Other plans, however, had been made for us temporarily. As a new replacement crew, it was necessary to prepare for active combat flying.

Combat flying was different from our previous training. The missions were almost always at very high altitudes requiring constant use of oxygen. The B-17G's were modified for combat which made the combat-ready B-17's fly *"heavy"* with changed performance. Most of all, missions were flown at icy temperatures near 50-60 degrees F below zero. In addition, close formation flying with heavy bomb loads at elevated altitudes was a chore. There were many features about combat to learn.

Orders were cut. B*rown's Crew* was assigned to the 401ˢᵗ Bomb Squadron, one of four Bomb Squadrons that comprised the 91st Bomb Group. Our arrival was late in the afternoon and was spent accumulating baggage and setting up quarters. The following morning our orders were amended to assignment to the 324ᵗʰ Bomb Squadron. The 324ᵗʰ Bomb Squadron had suffered heavy aircraft and aircrew losses the previous day on a tough mission to Bremen, Germany. This was our final move through the duration of air combat in the ETO.

The Bomb Group is divided into four Bomb Squadrons. The strength of the 91st Bomb Group was ordinarily 96 full combat aircrews with 24 in each Bomb Squadron. With three decimating visual bombing missions to Hamburg and to Bremen, and a return visit to Hamburg, aircrew strength in the 91st Bomb Group had dropped to approximately 62. This was barely enough for a full Group formation, after discounting aircrew combat casualties.

The 322nd, the 323rd, the 324th, and the 401st, made up the constituent Bomb Squadrons in the 91st Bomb Group. Shortly after *D-Day* the 324th Bomb Squadron had been reactivated into a standard Squadron from a blind (radar) bombing Squadron. Even as a new replacement crew, we found ourselves treated as veterans *before we began*. Less than five full veteran combat crews remained out of the newly reorganized 324th Bomb Squadron—five aircrews, instead of 24 combat aircrews.

Listing the Command: 324th Bomb Squadron Commanding Officer (CO) was Lt. Colonel Weitzenfeld; Adjutant, Major Krueger; Operations Officer, Capt. Dibble; and Asst. Operations Officer, Capt. Westfall. Commanding Officer of the 91st (H) Bomb Group was Colonel Terry; Dep. Commanding Officer, Lt. Colonel Milton; Group Operations Officer, Lt. Col. Sheiler; Group Bombardier, Capt. Hudson; Intelligence and Briefing Officer, Major Reid.

On the day of assignment to the 324th Bomb Squadron, the Commanding Officer of our Squadron, Lt. Col. Weitzenfeld, spoke to us briefly and made known his expectations. He inquired about our experience and background of training. After hearing us out, he outlined a program of indoctrination and made comments to this effect, "Well, men, you are new, so we will fly each of the replacement first pilots as co-pilots with an experienced veteran combat pilot for five missions. Then you will fly your own crew if you are found qualified to assume the responsibilities. Furthermore, if possible, due to our recent losses and preponderance of new unseasoned crews, we will attempt to send you out on picked targets that are easier than normal to get a feel of combat flying. You must understand that combat flying is different from any flying you have done, so pay attention, adjust yourself and learn quickly." We had listened intently—he dismissed us.

The Group formation in use at this time was the 54-plane formation. Three 18-plane units comprised the full Group formation. The *Lead* 18-plane unit led the entire Group formation of 54 planes, and flew in a relative position at the center of the whole assemblage. The second 18-plane formation was made up similarly and flew above and slightly to the rear and right of the Lead Group formation. The third 18-plane formation, organized as the other two formations, flew below and slightly to the rear and left of the Lead formation.

We flew a few minutes of close formation in borrowed aircraft later that same afternoon and examined newly installed modifications, which were unfamiliar. Our flight was short and restricted within sight of our field of operation, since we were unfamiliar with the terrain. One airfield in the ETO surprisingly resembled every other field.

That evening a recapitulation of new replacement crews assigned to the 324th Bomb Squadron reached six: Lt. Collins, Lt. Crans, Lt. O'Brien, Lt. Sherrill, and F/O Bessola, as well as mine.

Although the outlined schedule of indoctrination called for several more days of training, two of the new replacement crews were to become so-called veterans in one mission of combat. This was an experience that is indelibly inscribed in their memories.

"Triangle "A" Planes of Fame"

That Mystic Code

Obviously code was an absolute necessity for security reasons. Code was designed to prevent the enemy from obtaining timely information about identity and details of operation. It mostly prevented the enemy from advance knowledge of the mission. Code was particularly baffling to new replacement crews, since it was not only the code, but the protocol that was associated with it. Various methods and systems were used, but mainly fictitious names and alphabetical letters were used.

Each (H) Heavy Bombardment B-17G was a separate unit that was easily identified by alphabetic code——no two aircraft had the same combinations.

The 8th Air Force (H) Heavy Bombardment units were divided into three Divisions——First Division, Second Division, and Third Division. The First and Third Divisions flew B-17's while the Second Division flew B-24's. Each Division operated from a certain English locale in which all the component Bomb Groups were situated. Each Base was assigned a fictitious name, and no two Bases had identical names.

I will list a few code names and insignia for clarification:

- **First Division – Triangle on tail.** △
- **Second Division – Circle on tail.** ○
- **Third Division – Square on tail.** □

A letter identifying the Bomb Group appeared inside the triangle, circle, or square. The 91st Bomb Group had a Triangle with an "A" on the tail. Each Squadron within a Bomb Group had two letters inscribed on the side of the fuselage and all aircraft from any one Squadron bore these two letters. For example, the:

- **324th Bomb Squadron** – "DF" referred to by radio with the code name *Dimple*. All 324th aircraft were *Dimple* aircraft.
- **322nd Bomb Squadron** – "LF" and *Lingers*
- **323rd Bomb Squadron** – "OR" and *Ushers*
- **401st Bomb Squadron** – "MF" and *Mutters*

Each aircraft within a Squadron furthermore bore an alphabetical letter after the two-letter Squadron designation, such as "DF-R" or "DF-B" or "LF-Y" or "MF-C."

Other code names were as follows:

- **91st Bomb Group Formation** – Referred to as *Swordfish*
- **91st Bomb Group Landing Field** – Referred to as *Front piece*
- **Combat Wing** – For weather or instructions call *Fig Leaf*
- **Ground Sector Control** – For information on other formations call *Colgate*
- **Initial Point** – The point at which a formation initiates a bombing run on a target is referred to as the "IP."
- **Recall** – If conditions were such that the Command wished a formation or Force to return and abandon the mission, a typical recall would be the reference to four words, as *Red-Town-Dance-Tonight*.

There were innumerable other codes and names. In general, these above-mentioned code names were the most relevant to us.

On our first experience in combat, our first mission, we were confused and vaguely disconcerted by reference to code names, and we were generally unfamiliar with all the procedures that followed.

8ᵀᴴ AIR FORCE PATCH

8th Air Force and 9th Air Force

Actually the 8th Air Force and the 9th Air Force operated on different principles. The 8th Air Force was called a *Strategic* Air Force, since its targets were primarily targets of strategy —damage to enemy production and supplies, destruction of enemy airfields, enemy railway yards and harbor installations, oil refineries, and oil depots. The damage inflicted often manifested itself months after the bombing, but, nevertheless, it was a worthy and necessary contribution to Allied overall strategy and planning.

The 9th Air Force was a *Tactical* Air Force, dealing with immediate support of the Armies. Support of Allied troops, destruction of enemy equipment, supply depots, arterial approaches, and keeping enemy aircraft from molesting our troops, were all part of the tasks assigned to the 9th Air Force. The job was well done, as many a "GI Joe" will confirm.

The operations of the 8th Air Force and the 9th Air Force, although different in nature, were the air arm of the Army. The 8th Air Force and the 9th Air Force were the striking air blows that contributed to the final capitulation of the Nazis.

Both the 8th and 9th Air Force provided fighter "air cover" and often escort to the Strategic Bombers (H) as deep-penetration bombing missions into Germany proceeded.

Who Says When and Where and Why

I never cease to wonder at the task of finite planning that was essential for the successful culmination of a combat mission that perhaps involved upwards of 1,000 aircraft—the integration, the completeness of it all. It was an enormous undertaking and ably accomplished.

Target-selection protocol began strangely enough in Germany itself. Assessment of German resources was a critical factor. The most vital and important German resources supporting the German military forces must be destroyed. A group of industrial experts and strategy specialists provided information that assisted the Air Forces in prioritizing German targets. Reconnaissance and other information, some of it covert, also assisted mission and target selection.

A short distance from London, in the Teddington district, a group of buildings housed the unit called the United States Strategic and Tactical Air Force, known as USSTAF. The USSTAF Command Post was the nerve center for both the 8th Air Force and 9th Air Force. In code, this unit was referred to as *Wide Wing*, and *The Pit* was a bombproof operations office.

The beginnings of the combat mission started in USSTAF. It was here that the target was finally selected, the Air Force necessary for target destruction determined, integration and coordination of the Air Force specified, and essential mission details enumerated.

From USSTAF the information passed to the 8th and 9th Air Force Headquarters.

From the 8th Air Force Headquarters, code name *Pine Tree*, more details were accumulated, and the total information was forwarded through the secret TWX system to the relevant Bomb Groups. Upon receipt of the mission facts, the Bomb Groups further disseminated the information to their operating Squadrons. The able aircrews were then assigned.

The combat mission was born.

B-17G Air Combat Conditions

Tragedy and glamour of air combat sagas in B-17's during World War II often veils the hardship and unpleasant conditions that prevailed in each mission. The B-17G was primarily a long-distance, high-altitude heavy bomber that was used for the deep penetrations into Germany, and everywhere else to destroy significant targets. Missions therefore were normally made at 25000 feet or higher with the extraordinary low temperatures that prevail at that altitude. At altitudes, oxygen was required for extended periods to sustain life, and extreme care was necessary to prevent freezing and/or frostbite.

The B-17G was not a heated aircraft, although it had positions, such as pilot and co-pilot areas that had electric heating outlets for heated (wired) clothing. Temperatures at altitude were often in the minus 50 degrees Fahrenheit area, which means almost "instant freezing" when exposed to this environment, the flights at altitude often lasted for hours.

All aircrew wore heavy winter clothing to protect themselves and heavy-duty gloves to protect hands and fingers. In addition cold metal flak helmets and comparatively heavy flak-protectors were worn in actual air combat. When combined with a parachute, all this clothing made flight operations difficult, since often dexterity and body movement were required. Radio headsets over the helmet and about the ears provided a means for intercom and radio messages. Movement was constrained by limits of the oxygen mask outlets and the mask itself. The oxygen mask fit closely about the nose and mouth and was strapped to the head and B-17G oxygen lines provided outlets to plug the oxygen mask into the oxygen supply. The masks were generally uncomfortable when worn for hours, since pure oxygen had a drying effect and often caused blisters and sores. Frequent use of pure oxygen as well as exposure of oxygen to tender facial parts was a worry. It was general practice to start using oxygen at 12000 feet where pure oxygen was mixed with ambient outside air in an "Auto mix". "Auto mix" automatically adjusted to pure oxygen at altitudes over 18000 feet, or so. Radio and intercommunications capability were fitted in the oxygen mask assembly or in a throat microphone to enable speech and radio talk. When the final combat flying outfit was complete, the airmen were bundled, somewhat awkward assembly of body, body protection, equipment, and tubes and wires and straps.

My crew had several bouts with frostbite when protecting the B-17G from enemy fighters. When tracking the fighters with the movable 50 caliber machine guns in the waist area, there was body and facial exposure to dehydrating and freezing air flow. The frostbite was not extensive and/or disfiguring, however to either of the waist gunners. As mentioned elsewhere in this manuscript, I also lost part of the palm of my right hand when I was forced to remove my gloves to adjust oscillating autopilot movement. As the B-17 started to lose speed, I reached up and grabbed the speed quadrant – the palm of my hand immediately froze on the quadrant. Removing it required wrenching the hand from the quadrant, leaving flesh and blood on the controls.

In future wars, it is likely that clothing and equipment will be automated and designed to prevent the hardships encountered in World War II. It also may be that future wars will require different measures and equipment. The foregoing account of clothing, oxygen and use of the B-17G oxygen equipment is the best we had at that time so it was what we used. Hopefully it enhances the readers understanding that World War II, B-17G air operations were dangerous and awkward in many other aspects than actual combat and not always comfortable.

This Is What A Combat Mission Is Like

Most of our combat missions followed a general fundamental pattern. There were variations, but these variations were caused by weather, target defenses, and unforeseen conditions. These conditions happened, while not often, with regularity.

Usually by 2200 hours each evening Bomb Squadrons had submitted to Group Headquarters a list of available crews and the positions they were qualified to fly by combat experience or talent. Of these crews, those most likely to be called upon were alerted. Whether the mission was to be flown or not, these lists were forwarded faithfully as routine.

Alerted crews usually tried to get sleep early, since a mission starts in the middle of the night. The alert Officer or orderly wakens the crews when the mission is finally verified. Dressing quickly, the crews file out into the night to the mess hall for a swallow of coffee, a short breakfast, and then on to the briefing.

Generally, the Officers were briefed separately from the Enlisted Men, since the Officers were concerned with their position in the formation, codes, targets, routes, and similar information. The Enlisted Men, mostly gunners, were primarily concerned with anticipated enemy fighter opposition, rounds of ammunitions to be carried, firing information and the like. Radio Operators, however, were briefed individually for code instructions, radio calls and reports, and security measures. After the briefings, in the equipment dressing room, the crews finally collected as a unit.

Briefing rooms usually are closed rooms restricted only to authorized personnel, restricted even to personnel on the Field. The room itself included a wall-size map of England and the European Continent with a screen obscuring the target until the briefing began. Chairs faced the map. On the sidewall were two huge blackboards. One designated the formation and position of each plane and pilot; the other listed the combat codes. At the stipulated time, briefing began. The target was announced and routes examined. Methods to locate and identify the target, the bomb load, and other specific information were specified. Times were announced when crews were to be *at station*, *engines to be started*, *taxi time*, and *takeoff time*. Any and all questions were answered at this time. After the conclusion of briefing, the crews walked in small groups out into the night to the equipment room to dress for the mission.

Valuables were checked. Electrically heated flying-suits, gloves, flying boots, *Mae Wests* (inflatable life-preserver vests which can be inflated for suspension in the water), helmets, parachutes, and the metal flak helmets were put on. After dressing, the crew would invariably gather together for a last cigarette, a few jokes and comments, and a bit of nervous laughter while awaiting transportation to the plane. After arriving at the plane, equipment and armor were checked, personal equipment was loaded, and the crew was set *at station*. At prescribed times, the engines were started and planes taxied. With a *green-light* from the caravan (a portable command unit placed adjacent to the runway strip) throttles go forward, brakes are released, and 65000 pounds of vibrating metal, bombs, flesh and gasoline move forward and down the runway out of sight into darkness.

You Mean *Me*

Smug and satisfied that all was well, or as well as could be expected, I made a short flight in the local area. Later, I went to bed. I had hardly closed my eyes when I was wakened by someone tapping my shoulder. Turning over on my side, I directed a "What-da-ya-want?" in the general direction of a shaded flashlight.

A voice out of the darkness queried, "Are you Lt. Brown?" I countered rather brusquely, "Yes, I'm Brown, but what do you want?" The voice, again, "Lt. Brown, breakfast at 2400, briefing at 0100." The voice continued, "You're out today!" I pondered—it couldn't be true—I haven't completed my orientation courses——I'm not ready for a combat mission—the Commanding Officer said so! Then it dawned on me, as I directed my comment to the voice, "You have the wrong guy; you have the wrong Lt. Brown. Now go away, and let me sleep."

The flashlight drew nearer, flashed in my face, and the orderly—I could see him now—said, "No mistake, I have the right Lt. Brown. Lt. Collins is *out* today too."

What I didn't know about combat was fated to be learned by actual experience.

A Situation Has Developed

I think I shall always remember the unusual manner in which we began our first combat mission and the experiences that followed. I'm certain now that a *Power* more instrumental than ours guided us on our first mission to the target and back safely, for we were totally unprepared for the task. We were so naïve in our outlook - so very inexperienced in it all!

Our first mission began on the morning of the 21st of June 1944, as the orderly wakened us with the information, "Breakfast at 2400; briefing at 0100!"

The Commanding Officer of the 324th Bomb Squadron had previously advised us that, as replacement First Pilots, we would fly our first five missions as co-pilots without our own aircrew. My entire aircrew had been alerted and Lt. Collins' aircrew, as well. Inexperienced as I was, it was beyond my present comprehension that I would fly my first combat mission with my complete aircrew.

I dressed quickly, and with Lt. Collins, filed silently to the mess hall to eat, more absorbed in my own thoughts and speculations than in the food I swallowed tastelessly. As briefing time 0100 hours drew near, Lt. Collins and I walked the short distance in the night air to the briefing room and entered with a carelessness that belied our excitement, our feelings inside.

Small groups were standing about conversing in low tones. Lt. Collins and I, as First Pilots of the two replacement crews, attempted to appear casual and looked the situation over. We saw the covered wall-size map at the end of the briefing room, the blackboards, and our eyes simultaneously picked out, at the bottom of the formation, two names, Lt. Brown in "DF-E" and Lt. Collins in "DF-M". We still could not believe we were flying as First Pilots. We were naïve and incredulous, so new, we didn't know from —-, and we were unprepared and taken unaware. Our Commanding Officer, Lt. Col. Weitzenfeld, saw us and beckoned us over. We complied quickly. With a slight grin that perhaps belittled the expression in his eyes, he started with, "Fellows, I guess I was a little wrong. A situation has developed, and we had no alternative. Of the new replacement crews, you two were selected to fly this mission. We felt your records indicated that you have the best chance to get through successfully. Listen slowly, and if you have questions, out with them. I'll help you as much as I can, for some of this briefing may be new to you" - a masterful piece of understatement!

We soon learned how very little we knew. We had combat theory, but practical application was a different matter. I spoke up; "Whom are we co-piloting for, Colonel?" He replied, "That's what I mean, fellows, you both are taking your complete crews today. It's one of those things. It can't be helped. Our formation is short two crews, and the *"fill-ins"* for those two crews are you and Collins."

Briefing was called promptly at 0100 hours—efficiency was the keynote from here on—and the Colonel walked away with a, "I'll see you both after briefing."

Lt. Collins, whom I called *"Collie,"* turned to me and smiled. "Brownie," he said, "I'm glad we're going out together. We'll sweat this one out. It's probably an easy mission; you remember what the Commanding Officer said." I replied, "Sure, "Collie". They don't send new replacement aircrews on rough missions on their first trip. I also remember what the Commanding Officer said." I wondered later if I really believed it.

The screen came up on the wall-size map to reveal the target. A moan reverberated throughout the room as we noticed the target – Berlin, *Big-B*, the center of the city,

<u>Wilhelmstrasse Railway Station</u>. I turned around to see a sickly grin on Collie's face – I think I grinned too, but it was habit and not a grin of feeling. I thought sarcastically, "<u>Yes, an easy mission, all right – real easy</u>!"

Briefing continued in rapid progression from one fact to the next. "Collie" and I scribbled feverishly in our notebooks. The lights would go out, then, turn on, and as briefing drew to a conclusion, I glanced at my notes to see the conglomeration of names, letters, and hieroglyphics. I turned to "Collie" with a, "Collie", do you know about all this stuff?"

Lt. Collins grinned and returned, "No, guess I missed a couple of ground school classes somewhere along the line."

I felt the same way—lost in the rapid progression of events. The Commanding Officer came our way, and asked, "Have you got any questions, fellows?" I thought, "Is he kidding?" And he continued on with, "We'll have to keep moving. We haven't much time from here on. We can talk on the way to the equipment room."

We asked a few questions as we walked out in the darkness to the equipment dressing room, but we were so mixed up – so confused. We naturally held back, determined to play the part as best we knew it.

The equipment room was quiet, as it always was, when the mission was expected to be a rough one. At this time, Berlin was considered the top of the list of places combat crews wished to avoid.

We dressed quickly. Shortly, we gathered together, and the Colonel took both our crews to our respective planes. We dropped Lt. Collins' aircrew at his plane. I remember seeing an old war-battered plane with a name, *The Ruptured Duck*, boldly inscribed and aptly illustrated on the nose. My plane loomed out of the darkness, and the Commanding Officer offered a, "Well, I'll be damned! Whoever assigned this plane? This is the unmodified B-17G plane that was flown in yesterday." It was a new B-17G, but obviously it was unmodified—the deicer boots were still installed on the wings. Deicer boots were always removed in combat conditions. If flak penetrated the rubber deicer boots, they would balloon out, making the aircraft difficult to control. A quick check of the bomb load indicated we carried time-bombs with short fuses. This brought out another torrent of expletives from the Commanding Officer. He contacted Armament, and in no uncertain terms asked how long it would take to reload the bomb racks, but the task was out of the question.

So there it was! A further examination indicated that certain armor plate had not yet been installed, and no flakvests were provided. Moreover, the machine guns would not fit in the bracket mounts. Finally with the aid of mallets, sweat, and muscle, the flexible machine guns were installed. We hoped they worked—the guns were new and unmodified. We loaded our equipment, adjusted ourselves, and we were finally set. Engine time drew near, so we fired up and waved in the darkness in the general direction where we'd left the Commanding Officer, and then prepared to taxi.

We hadn't the slightest idea where we were located on the Base—the air field. It was the late black darkness that precedes the dawn, and lights were unauthorized for security reason. So, as a black shadow materialized out of the darkness, apparently on the way to the take-off strip, we followed. If that black shadow had been a lorry on the way to London, I probably would have followed it. We were lost on our own Field, unaware of the direction to taxi, and just generally in the dark. I learned later that Lt. Collins made the same decision, an obvious one, of course. We tagged the rest of the planes. When the aircraft in front of us pulled sluggishly on the runway for take-off, we pulled out right behind, and on the "green light" pushed the throttles forward and headed down an indistinct and unlighted runway. I just took off – took off on the heading I happened to be on—you couldn't see any outline of the runway.

Our instructions were to climb on a heading of 235 degrees magnetic until we reached 12,000 feet, then turn around and fly 055 degrees magnetic back to our Base. Assembly was at 20,000 feet on a radio fix over the Base—red-red flares would indicate our Group formation.

As we turned back, daylight was filtering through a high overcast from the east. The crew was chattering, oblivious to the seriousness of the mission. We were still under the opiate of anticipation of our first combat mission - heading into long awaited combat for the first time. Knowing that approximately 1,200 (H) Heavy Bombers were out in the Force this day, we expected the sky literally to be filled with aircraft, but as we looked about, the sky appeared empty with the exception of one lone B-17G

A cloud layer obscured the ground. Our new B-17G did not have the combat navigational equipment installed—I learned later that Lt. Collins' plane had the equipment, but it was relatively inoperative. With this in mind, I identified from the distance that the lone B-17G we had sighted had a triangle with an "A" inscribed on the tail. We knew it was a 91st Bomb Group aircraft. We varied our course slightly to intersect the course of this other plane. Strangely enough, the other plane turned toward us. As we both picked up our original courses, we were flying practically wing to wing. We examined the other aircraft more closely. It was The Ruptured Duck with Lt. Collins and his crew. We waved, dipped our wing, and headed on toward the point of assembly.

I remembered figuring, "Perhaps "Collie" knows where he's going, and so I'll just fly along and let him lead me to the formation." As we reached 20,000 feet, we saw in the distance two bright red flares drifting down from a formation – our identification flares, so therefore our formation. I thanked our luck for finding "Collie" and his subsequent help in locating the formation. Lt. Collins came to me after the mission and said, "Brownie", I don't think I'd ever have found the formation if I hadn't followed you." As a matter of fact, we had both followed each other, and inadvertently stumbled luckily on the correct formation. God just looks after those who can't look after themselves. We were in good fortune that day and subsequent days after that.

We joined the formation at the tail end, at the bottom of the formation, a position we later learned was dubbed, "*Purple-Heart Corner*." "Purple-Heart Corner" was perhaps the most vulnerable spot in the entire formation. This was the spot where enemy fighters usually attacked first, since the lightest formation firepower could be directed against them. I was flying the outside of the Vee formation with Lt. Collins, the inside. We had no idea at the time of the likely casualty prospects inherent in our "Purple Heart Corner" formation position. I know now the meaning of the expression,—"*Ignorance is bliss!*"We exchanged waves as we climbed across the English Channel, Denmark, and the North Sea till we reached 25,000 feet bombing altitude.

We had an unopposed trip until we reached 100 miles from Berlin. The radio suddenly announced: "Bandits in the area. Bandits in the area." That expression meant nothing to us at the time. The formation tightened, and the turrets quickened their sweeps of the sky. We learned later that *Bandits* was code for enemy fighters. A collection of black dots representing German fighters appeared on the horizon from a position where *3 o'clock* would appear on a mantle timepiece. As the black dots came closer, they appeared as a swarm of bees flying with no apparent formation at all. I switched from radio to interphone and passed on the information with a few instructions to the crew. I was pleased to hear the crew calling out the enemy fighters, clearing the 50-caliber machine guns, and demonstrating practiced disciplines. The turrets were tracking the enemy fighters as they circled to the rear of our whole formation. Suddenly the tail-gunner called out, "Here they come, 6 o'clock level!" The first Luftwaffe fighter pass was made, as expected, at the low formation "Purple-Heart Corner." The B-17G ahead of us, our leader, suddenly caught fire, started flaming, and nosed down. Lt. Collins and I pulled ahead to the next forwardformation, doing all kinds of aero-gymnastics to destroy the aim of the enemy fighters attacking us.. Guns rattled, interphone conversation sporadically cut in reporting both FW-190 and ME-109 German plane fighter attacks. I switched over to radio, designating the co-pilot to monitor interphone, just in time to hear the plea, "Little Friends, Little Friends, Swordfish formation under enemy attack; 80 miles northwest of Point "B"; I repeat..." – and the same message.

Out of somewhere came the reply, "Big Friends, Big Friends, Swordfish Formation. Hold tight; we have you sighted; we'll give you a hand!" The *Little Friends*, of course, were friendly fighter aircraft. The *Big Friends* were the American (H) Heavy Bombers.

The enemy fighters, as if sensing the situation, made a final mass attack from the side and rear. Three B-17G bombers, in different formations ahead of us, caught fire, and flaming, dropped out of the formation. The "ball" turret gunner reported that one of the B-17G's exploded several thousand feet below us. The other two bombers, flaming and out of control, fell earthward. One B-17G seemed momentarily to gain control, go into a wild loop, and then continue earthward. No parachutes were seen coming from the doomed and flaming B-17G aircraft.

As sudden as the attack, the enemy fighters - the Bandits - were gone; and our Little Friends passed swiftly overhead in chase. I think there is a place in every bomber crewman's heart reserved for our Little Friends who so often gave us a hand when a situation developed.

We were nearing the initial turning point (IP) for the target. We were beginning to realize that this mission, like others, would cause men to die, and B-17G's to be destroyed— the smooth metal of the Flying Fortress marked with shrapnel and bullet holes.

The bombing formation turned to the heading that would take us directly to Berlin. The formation tightened. In the distance a dark cloud appeared. The cloud, man-made from 75mm, 105mm, and 155mm exploding anti-aircraft shells, was spewing death and destruction among those who would dare to enter—German retribution for the damage that would be done to Berlin.

Bombers in the formation drop bombs on a signal from the Lead aircraft, unless briefing varied the routine. No bomber breaks formation during a bomb run. A bomb release formation is important. Each B-17G formation bomb-load is released where it will do the most damage on impact.

The first bombers disappeared in the flak cloud. Our bomb-bay doors were opened—I advanced throttles to compensate for the increased drag.

Evasive action to disturb the aim of the German gunners began - turns to the left and right, as the first bursts of flak barraged our units. Soon the puffs of black and white smoke became dense and flak whistled through the aircraft.

The "Bomb run is on!"

The formations align in trail, the "bomb run" heading is adjusted, and the formation straightens out level at the IP for the 60 seconds of the "bomb run." All evasive action is discarded now. Bombs on target are the important motivating objective now.

A B-17G in front of us, suddenly received a direct flak hit. The B-17G broke into two sections—both sections fell earthward, spinning rapidly. Another B-17G, directly ahead of us, pulled out to the left, losing altitude with a damaged engine smoking. Lt. Collins and I pulled ahead in the formation. Suddenly, the Lead B-17G, at the vertex of the entire formation disgorged its bombs—*"bombs away!"* The entire formation simultaneously released their bombs. Approximately 300,000 pounds of high explosive began a one-way journey into Berlin, Germany. We observed that bombing accuracy—it was excellent— later verified from bomb-release photographs.

Bomb-bays closed, throttles retarded, and wild, wonderful evasive action resumed. The last instructions I remember from the Commanding Officer was "Follow the Lead Pilot at all times and do what he does. You'll make it through!"

After "bombs away", the Group formation quickly reorganized.

Suddenly, our new V-formation leader pulled up sharply in a climb through the entire low formation. Well, orders were orders, so Lt. Collins and I both followed on his wings in formation. He leveled out finally, high and to the right of the Low Squadron with us both still in formation with him.

There we were—in the vicinity of Berlin, Bandits in the area, and in a lonely three-plane V- formation. Our formation leader seemed to get his B-17G under control and headed back to rejoin the Group formation. We were lucky that day, for we regained our Group formation without mishap. We learned later that the elevator controls of the B-17G had been damaged. Out of control, the aircraft had gone into a climb. The automatic pilot was engaged, with its separate controls, and our V-formation leader brought his aircraft under control in this manner.

The remainder of the trip home was relatively uneventful as we crossed the enemy coast, the English Channel, and approached the English coast. Over the Channel, however, several B-17G's dropped from Group formation with battle damage. Again our Little Friends hovered about to see them back safely.

The ground was obscured over England by a heavy undercast cloud layer that extended partially over the channel. As we reached a specific spot, apparently a radio beacon, each B-17G in the formation executed a prescribed maneuver—that is, all B-17G's but DF-E, my aircraft, and DF-M, Lt. Collin's aircraft. The Group formation, except for us, descended into the clouds and disappeared in what we learned later was a "let-down" procedure used to penetrate solid undercast cloud layers. Lt. Collins and I knew nothing of any "let-down" procedure. When our lead B-17G aircraft headed into the clouds, we couldn't imagine flying close formation with such limited visibility, so we remained above the clouds.

There we were, Collie and me, in two B-17G's, somewhere over England. We would "start" a mission and "end it" the same way—lost! What a day of experiences!

Finally Lt. Collins turned in one direction, I in the other, and both of us "let-down" through the clouds in opposite directions. As I came out of the clouds we circled trying to locate Lt. Collins, but visibility was poor. We apparently had lost him. For about 45 minutes we tried to pick up landmarks, but in England, the airfield, and the towns and rivers all bear a remarkable similarity. Eventually we resorted to a method known in code as "QDM" which gave us a radio bearing from ground units to our Base. We arrived at what must be our Base and approached for landing. As we dropped our wheels and landing flaps, another B-17G, slightly ahead of us, touched down on the runway for landing. We landed and rolled down the runway and turned off at the end. We then recognized the B-17G ahead of us as Lt. Collins and The Ruptured Duck.

The Base seemed deserted, and for all practical purposes nearly was, for we were an hour late. We both taxied around the edge of the field and finally parked the two B-17G's—we hadn't the slightest idea where they belonged. We visited for several minutes and with exhilaration, unloaded our equipment and walked back to the equipment room—even transportation had gone home.

We undressed, then redressed, picked up our secret papers and equipment, walked the short distance to Squadron operations, rapped once, and walked in.

The 324th Squadron Operations' Officer, Capt. Dibble, glanced up, performed a true double—take, and remarked elatedly, "This can't be! Both of you were reported lost over the target! You were shot down!"

"Collie" and I looked at each other, grinned, and I replied, "Captain, we just landed!" and continued, "Where do you want us to put this stuff?" indicating the equipment we were both carrying.

The Operations Officer just shook his head and nodded, "You two! We had given you up for lost. Just drop the stuff here. I'll take care of it for you. Better get some food and get some sleep."

We complied, turned, and as we left the operations office, we noticed two blank spaces on the blackboard that listed Squadron crew personnel – black empty spaces where our names had been before.

Our first combat mission was completed.

"BOMB-BAY DOORS OPENING TO DROP BOMBS"

BOMBS AND BOMBING

"THE FACT IS THAT I NEVER EVEN THOUGHT ABOUT IT, UNTIL—-!"

Most veteran bomb pilots that carried live ordnance in combat missions were preoccupied with details of mission execution and combat flying disciplines. Sitting astride several tons of high explosives in your bomb-bay with bombs fuzed to explode upon impact was more of an "aside" than a fear. An "aside", that is, until in flight, the B-17G in combat formation, in front of your aircraft, during an approach to a target under heavy anti-aircraft fire (flak) suddenly disappears in a huge yellow, orange, and red pyrotechnic burst. A momentary drifting black and white cloud appears where there should be an aircraft. One or more of the thousands of red-hot pieces of flak had penetrated and exploded the fuel tank or detonated a bomb in the B-17G bomb-bay.Fuselage parts from the exploding aircraft hit your windshield and dent or pierce the aircraft body. It was an instant in time that emotions over loss of a combat crew and the deadly threat of a "not yet delivered" bomb payload is an event that will ever be remembered. Soon the bombs are "away", the bomb-bay doors are closed, and a new threat of staying alive during an upcoming fighter attack overwhelms attention. The memory persists, however, and an element of more concern enters the psyche as new missions occur.

Bombs varied in design and fuzing and purpose.The most common ordnance was the General Purpose (GP) 500 pound gravity bomb. The heaviest bomb that I carried in the bomb-bay in my missions was a 2000 pound penetrating bomb designed to destroy concrete installations, submarine pens, concrete docks, and large underground installations. Other bombs of varying weights included fragmentation bombs for supply areas, troop concentrations, and other installations. Incendiary bombs were sometimes carried by following formations to ignite the rubble caused by the first onslaught of exploding ordnance.

The B-17G bomb-bay was a large open compartment located mid-ship the aircraft, with a catwalk through the center to allow passage through the bomb-bay. Bomb release hangers (racks) were suspended from the top of the bomb-bay or from the side to hold the ordnance (bombs) in place until released. Bomb-bay doors opened and closed from each side.

All the bombs during my missions were gravity bombs. It was interesting to note that the bombs when first released remained somewhat under and slightly behind the releasing aircraft until air resistance (air drag) caused them to gradually move rearward as they dropped. The drop patterns expanded slightly as they dropped— gradually the bombs were out of sight. Bombs could be released "all at once" or, in sequence, by an intervalometer.

Often during the formation recovery after bomb release, the formation maneuvered to the left or right to reassemble the formation. This maneuver allowed visual sight of the explosions occurring on the target.

The fuzing process varied. Most bombs were fuzed "safe' until entering enemy areas. Most fuzing was two-stage. The first stage was a small air-stream propeller held in place on each bomb by a pin that could be removed. After the pin was removed, the second stage allowed the small propeller to spin off, thereby arming the impact fuze.

The most important issue beyond crew safety in the bombing issue was the formation bomb patterns. In most Group combat formations, three Squadrons, (lead), (high), and (low), representing 36 or 54 aircraft in Vee formation would approach a target "run". At the "initial point" (IP) of the "run" the high and then low formations would form "in trail" of the leading Squadron to execute the 1-3 minute Group target approach. After "bombs away" the Squadrons would rapidly reform into the large Group formation. The purpose of all these maneuvers was to form an impact bomb pattern that would be most destructive to the target. The formation reforming was to provide protection against fighter aircraft in the target area.

The Bombardier was the B-17G bomb delivery and ordnance manager. The Norden Bombsight was the Secret weapon that was remarkably effective for high altitude visual bombing in World War 11. The Norden Bombsight was not just an instrument, but a bombing system. It was integrated with the B-17G autopilot and released the bombs. It was an optical electromechanical device that could "servo" aircraft direction in the last few minutes before bomb release. The pilot adjusted the autopilot for bomb run sensitivity and metrics, centered the PDI, and released the aircraft to the Bombardier and the Norden Bombsight. The Norden Bombsight usually was programmed before the mission to represent the factors affecting the bomb trajectory. Small changes in the factors could be made by the Bombardier in flight. At bombing time, the Bombardier centered the optical cross-hairs on the target and adjusted the Norden Bombsight to stop drift (side movement) and maintain azimuth (flight direction) to assure that misdirection didn't occur during the bomb flight which ultimately would impact five miles or so below on the target. At a precise moment, the bombs were released, and the B-17G was returned to the pilot. During my Command Lead efforts, only the Bombardier in the Lead Command aircraft and the Bombardier in the Second-in- Command B-17G carried the Norden Bombsight. The remaining Bombardiers manually "toggled" the release of their bombs simultaneously with the Lead aircraft.

Direct anti-aircraft (flak) hits or random penetration of pieces of flak on bombs in the Bomb-bay causing B-17G explosions did not occur on every mission. The frequency, however, was more often to occur on highly defended targets. In my thirty (30) combat missions, I probably sighted ten (10) B-17G explosions. It always created a demoralizing effect on the psyche due to the random nature and suddenness of the event and sadness for the lost crew.

Bombardiers often proclaimed that with a Norden Bombsight they could drop a bomb from 5 miles high into a "German pickle barrel".
Perhaps?

"B-17G Being Bombed From Above"

"CRITICAL TAIL SECTION BOMBED"

"Co-Pilot Takes a Bullet"

"Bomb-Bay" Hit

"Severed Tail Section"

Flak

The word, *flak*, appears frequently in this narrative. Many hear flak associated with anti-aircraft defenses and battle damage. Some may visualize mistakenly that anti-aircraft guns fire a single large bullet to intercept the aircraft, like a rifle shot. In fact, it more closely resembles a shotgun shot of 100-1000 large bullets.

Flak is a small irregular piece of metal that ranges in general size from one to three cubes of sugar. It is a fragment of an anti-aircraft shell that ranges in size from 88mm to 155mm in diameter. This equates approximately to a 3 to 6 inch diameter shell. The inner case of the bullet-part of the shell is scribed or etched to provide lines of weakness to define the size of fragmentation when the explosive detonates. The result is fragmentation of the shell into hundreds of small, hot, jagged parts that fly randomly in all directions.

The anti-aircraft shell is launched by a rapid-fire artillery piece. The shell can be timed to explode at a predetermined altitude, making it extremely versatile. The lethal area varies, but it was known to be effective for as much as 100 yards in range. Several of these flak shells can be fired in a minute, so an area can be flooded with flying lethal metal. The German defensive strategy varied with the target and the number of anti-aircraft weapons. There are times that accurate anti-aircraft fired only a few shots, and other times the strategy was to lay out a barrage of anti-aircraft shells that the invading aircraft had to fly through. The barrage technique was more frequently used on heavily defended targets.

The explosive charge was apparently black powder that left a distinctive symbolic black cloud-like pattern resembling a large molar tooth. During a barrage of anti-aircraft fire the sky would be so black that formations would literally disappear into the abyss.

The lethal flak fragments shredded the aircraft aluminum *skin* and control surfaces, punctured the windshields and plexiglas nose *greenhouses*, damaged engines, and most of all punctured the wing fuel tanks. The flak metal fragments were sufficiently hot to ignite fuel and unreleased bombs. When reference is made to battle damage, it most frequently meant shredded and broken aircraft parts, structure and engine areas penetrated by these flak fragments.

Aircrews were provided flak vests and helmets and sometimes armor plate in critical areas to protect against the flying metal. Flak was a major contributor to aircrew casualties. Make no mistake; flak was lethally dangerous.

As I hold several pieces of German flak in my hand (remnants from my own combat experience), it seems extraordinary that these little irregular metal pieces caused so much personal anguish and damage.

"FLAK"

Time Out

For the next three days we studied the many little things we should have known before our first mission, but didn't. By the time our next combat mission was scheduled, we had answers. Experience on our first mission to Berlin taught us the price of being unprepared. As replacement pilots, there were immense benefits in learning how to fly combat style. So we trained, practiced, and worked hard to learn combat skills.

On the evening of 24 June 1944, we were alerted for our 2nd mission. A letter from Lt. General Doolittle, Commander of the 8th Air Force, informed us that the tour of duty had been increased from 25 to 35 missions. Furthermore, all air crewmen with missions previous to the middle of June 1944 would be credited extra missions to adjust their tour of duty.

Early in the morning on the 25th of June 1944, our orderly awakened us. We proceeded with breakfast, briefing, and other details in routine fashion. By the time the sun was rising in the east we were heading out over the English Channel on a southerly route bound for southern France. Our target was an airfield near Toulouse, France. We learned at a later date that this was part of the softening process for the invasion strategy of our Forces in France.

The mission was without major incident, except for sporadic bursts of uncharted anti-aircraft fire as we progressed to the target. I had graduated to an *element leader*, so I had 2 wingmen. We turned on the bomb run, dropped our bombs with reasonably good results, and suffered slight flak damage as we left the target area. The flak was relatively light compared to our previous deep-penetration mission to Berlin. We noticed then, and later verified our observation that flak over France was usually lighter in intensity, but often very accurate.

Leaving the target area we headed out to sea to avoid bad weather that had been coded to us by radio. The weather was worse than anticipated, and we were driven far out to sea. Our gasoline supply was running low, so with no alternative, the formation headed into the weather, losing altitude as visibility became poor. Low-hanging clouds complicated formation flying. We were soon flying scarcely over the whitecaps. We suddenly came upon a battle fleet of warships. We pulled over the tops of the masts and disappeared in the mist and clouds.

We thanked our deliverance to a small secret electronic unit, called "IFF", which meant *"identification—friend or foe"*. Had this unit been inoperative, the naval warships would have been obliged to fire at us with perhaps catastrophic results. Finally weather became so bad the formation fell to pieces, and each plane was obliged to find its own way home. Many of the aircraft that were low on gasoline landed at other fields and returned the next day after refueling.

Except for the miserable weather, the remainder of the trip was without incident. We landed, were interrogated, and headed for the mess hall and sleep. It was a long mission, but it was successful, so we felt pleased.

Mission 2 was complete.

A Milk Run

While missions were flown the next two days, we were not scheduled to fly. We fretted, since the missions were easy French bridge targets, which meant light flak and short trips. We called this type of mission a *"milk run"*. We hated to miss the easy, short missions for obvious reasons.

On the evening of June 27, 1944 we were alerted for Mission 3. Early on the 28th of June 1944, we caught a "milk run" to Anizy, France. Our target was a bridge over which the Germans were running supplies to their troops in the Paris region. I had graduated again to Squadron Lead with five planes in formation behind me.

We missed our target by several hundred yards and the bridge was still intact when we left it; another formation directly behind us destroyed it, however. We were disappointed that our flight had not been successful. As punishment, the bombardiers dropped practice bombs on a practice range for two days.

Weather and Angels

With three missions accredited, we were on our way. With luck at this rate, barring mishap, we should make short order of our tour of combat duty. This was an optimistic view for a group of neophytes, but we were encouraged by the rapid progression of events. Three days later, early on the 30th of June, 1944, we were out again on a tough target - a significant industrial installation in Bremen, Germany.

Briefing instructions were to assemble over our usual "radio fix" at our field at 20,000 feet. In the equipment dressing room, supplemental instructions informed us that weather was anticipated. We were also told that the code name *angels*" and *"devils"* would be applied for any change in assembly altitude – "angels" for an increase in altitude, and "devils" for a decrease.

The mission was off successfully, and, as we climbed for assembly, we received radio instructions to assemble at three "angels" which would mean 23,000 feet. Another radio message advisory before we reached altitude instructed us to assemble at six "angels". By this time, the air was congested with aircraft milling about and circling over the "radio fix", so I instructed the crew to be on the lookout for any aircraft on a collision course. Visibility was atrocious, and not long thereafter we received radio instructions, "Swordfish Formation, assemble nine "angels". Up and up - climbing was more difficult now, since we were heavily loaded with bombs and gasoline. Our power settings were extreme, the engines were heating up, and the laboring engines were rapidly consuming our gasoline reserve.

At 28,500 feet we broke into the clear and noticed a few planes circling about in a semblance of a formation. Flying was difficult under the existing conditions. Our power settings were now extreme, far above average, but we joined formation. A check by the co-pilot indicated our fuel supply was barely within limits for the trip, and any delay would force us to abandon the mission due to gasoline shortage.

Other formations were in difficulty. Some planes were unable to gain the altitude with the loads, while others were already beyond safe fuel limits for the mission. It looked troublesome, but finally instructions from *Fig Leaf* were radioed to us in code, "George-Red-Tavern-Tonight," which meant that the mission was to be abandoned by the Force. All aircraft were to return to their respective Bases. We listened and turned back with a feeling of reprieve. Bremen, Germany was a dangerous and highly protected area. Its important industrial complexes were critical to the German war machine.

We would return another day!

Rest – Then Maximum Effort

Our assembly difficulties on the scheduled mission to Bremen on the 30th of June, 1944 precipitated an engineering headache. We had experienced more than usual mechanical trouble - high gasoline consumption, overheating engines, loss of power, and consequent inability to reach altitude. So for two days, working night and day, ground crews labored over our B-17G's. Although several short missions were scheduled, our crew sat out the missions, again bemoaning the fact that we always missed the easy ones. New replacement crews, however, gained experience on these missions and our formations in practice became fine-tuned and consistently compact.

For three days, the 91st Bomb Group sat on the ground. No missions were scheduled, although weather was good over England and the Continent. Speculation ran high—something "big in the making". Our premonitions were well founded. On the evening of the 10th of July, 1944, we were alerted for an "M-E," a maximum effort, where every commissionable aircraft flew. On the morning of the 11th of July, 1944, our briefed target was an industrial target in Munich, Germany – a grueling, long, and tough mission.

As we crossed over France bound for southern Germany, I remember a sight that made me realize the strength of our (H) Heavy Bomber striking force. As we winged into the east, into the sun, as far as the eye could reach, the sunlight glanced, amplified, and reflected off the gleaming silver metal of *Flying Fortresses*. Hundreds of minute light particles glistened and shimmered far into the horizon.

It was beautiful and was impressed in my memory. I saw the Swiss Alps that day for the first time. Though we were flying at 20,000 feet for the most part, the mountains seemed to reach up to us. It's strange and wondrous how far the eyesight can reach with excellent weather conditions, flying four, five, or six miles high. We finally initiated our climb to 25,000 feet, our bombing altitude. Our radio reported that several formations ahead were under enemy fighter attack. Shortly a flight of American P-51 *Mustangs* passed overhead to intercept the enemy fighters. Before *bombs away*, two B-17G's dropped out of formation with engines flaming. Munich was well-defended by anti-aircraft defenses. We suffered several hits to our aircraft, but no major damage was caused at the time.

Bombs were "*away*". As we turned off the target, we had a tight moment when flak apparently had zeroed in on our altitude and course. Our evasive action seemingly was anticipated, and damage became more serious than previously experienced on this mission. Ahead to the right, a direct flak hit crumpled the left wing of a Flying Fortress. As the wing detached, the B-17G spun slowly at first, then more rapidly. The good news was that several parachutes blossomed our far below as the plane gyrated earthward.

We were a tired aircrew as we returned from the long grind and eight hours on oxygen. Anti-aircraft had scored damage to our B-17G, *Miss Lucky*. The tail section was badly perforated, and a large section of the vertical stabilizer was missing. The rudder action was stiff and, apparently, the elevator section was damaged. There appeared to be an obstruction to movement of the elevators, since the aircraft was slow in response—this made flying close formation difficult and worried us about landing safely. Flak pieces also had penetrated our main gasoline tank, but the self-sealing feature had retained most of our fuel. We were able to hold formation loosely, although it was a struggle—damage was major. We returned to our Base and made a safe, but rough landing, in spite of the battle damage.

We didn't know then, but this was the beginning of three tiring days during which we accumulated over 28 hours of combat flying and over 24 hours on oxygen. With our assigned B-17G, Miss Lucky, undergoing repair, a new B-17G was assigned to our aircrew for the remaining missions to Munich, Germany

Mission 4 was complete.

Blitz

I remember details vaguely during the subsequent 48 hours - the 12th and 13th of July 1944. It was more a period of impressions than anything else; impressions of persistent orderlies waking us, briefings always targeting Munich, Germany, variations of "aiming points" with essentially the same routes, flying hour upon hour on oxygen, and physical exhaustion. The aircrew had scarcely ten hours sleep over the three days of long missions. During this blitz of Munich, fires blazed and smoldered for several weeks after our three days of terror. Tons of bombs rained from the skies as if this were the end of time and existence. I can only imagine the horror of being on the recipient end of our bomb cargoes of 500-pounders, of 1000-pounders, of time bombs set to explode at intervals up to a week hence, of our incendiary firebombs. At the end, Munich was a shambles. Our troops verified this fact when they entered the battered city at a later date.

Air casualties were heavy, as the enemy on the ground and in the air attempted to halt our obvious objective. Battle damage to our *Flying Fortresses* was a nightmare for our loyal ground crews. Working throughout the night, ground crews scarcely had re-commissioned a plane from the previous day's combat when it was in the air again. Even as the last fastener was twisted into place, the engines were turning over. Later, the same afternoon, the same aircraft was back on the hardstand parking space. Perhaps this time the aircraft had easily repairable damage. Then again, perhaps it was hardly recognizable as the same plane – deformed, with an engine, or two engines inoperative - engines barely hanging in engine mounts with metal ripped and torn.

This period was hard for us all, and not the least, the ground crews. Often the combat aircrews, tired, irritable, and quiet, seemed unappreciative of the effort required keeping these huge metal birds in the air. Often the aircrews walked silently away with scarcely a nod to the laboring ground crew - hardly a smile, or a casual backslap.

Our bombing was good on two of the missions, fair on the other, but the overall mission results were excellent. Not all combat crews flew three consecutive missions to Munich, but those who did were given notice that 48 hours leave was theirs - theirs to spend as they wished. My leave was spent in a soft comfortable bed in the Regent Palace Hotel in London with pleasant dining and "no briefings". I felt measurably better when I boarded the LMS Railway Train to Royston and Bassingbourn.

My leave was at an end and I was ready again to resume work.

"B-17G's in Flying Formation"

Formation Flying

The most important stratagem for protection of heavy bombers against the German Air Force, the Luftwaffe, was close formation flying. Deep penetrations to important industrial targets were often without our "Little Friend", fighter air support. The heavy bombers were most often attacked by fighters as they neared a target and again after "bombs away". Often bombers damaged by anti-aircraft "flak" were prime targets for the Luftwaffe, and few aircrews survived their vicious attacks.

Close formation flying was not generally taught in the United States flying program, so it was important to learn quickly in the combat area. Practice formation sessions were flown often to sharpen skills for actual air combat. While not popular, the practice sessions were insurance for survival. The first few missions of newly arrived aircrews were critical— survival depended on skills in air combat operations—practice helped.

The new aircrews started in the most dangerous position, "Purple Heart Corner" located at the low end of the massive formations of 54 bombers in late 1943 to mid 1944. In late 1944, formations of 36 bombers were flown in combat missions usually with fighter support. After starting in "Purple Heart Corner", aircrews progressed forward in the formation.

The traditional 54 bomber Group formation consisted of three (3) formations of 18 aircraft. The Lead 18 bombers flew center of the 54 bomber formation. The "high"

18 bombers flew above and to the right and trail of the Lead 18 bombers. The "Low" 18 bombers flew below and to the left and trail of the Lead 18 bombers. Often in World War II, the bomber fleet included as many as 1,200 heavy four-engine bombers.

In each of the three 18 bomber formations comprising the 54 plane bomb Group formation, "Lead", "High", and "Low" sub-formations are formed by 6 bombers in two 3 plane "Vee" formations, one 3 plane formation following the other. These 6 bomber "Vees" were arranged in traditional "Lead", "High" and "Low" assemblies to form sub-units of the total 54 plane bomber Group formations.

Assembling a fifty-four (54) Group Formation is a formidable task. There is always a lead aircraft in a traditional formation that forms a "point". The Lead Command Pilot is the first to take-off and climbs in a prescribed manner, to avoid collisions, to an assigned altitude over a radio "beacon". The Lead Command Pilot then initiates large circular courses (orbits) around the "beacon". Other aircraft take off and assume their relative assigned positions in the formation. As the final aircraft joins the formation, the Lead Command Pilot initiates a course to meet and "pick-up" another fifty our (54) Group Formation at a precise time and position. This process replicates itself until the entire bomber armada is formed "in trail". At this time, the Lead Command Pilot initiates the first leg of the combat route into Germany.

Each pilot learns to fly as a wingman, either left or right of the respective "point" lead aircraft in the 3 plane sub-elements of the total formation. The "point" or lead aircraft establishes a fixed heading at a fixed moderate speed at a fixed altitude. A wingman then approaches the wing tip of the lead aircraft and slowly edges forward to trail its wingtip closely at a slightly higher position. As the wingman approaches 50-100 feet of the lead aircraft's wing tip, the throttle is slowly decreased to achieve position and the throttle is adjusted to equate the forward motion of the lead aircraft. The wing aircraft pilot adjusts power to reduce the rate-of-change in the position of the lead aircraft's wing tip and his own wing tip. The wingman's aircraft is "trimmed" for ease of flying, and it is now in position. The other wingman, on the other side of the lead aircraft, replicates the maneuver.

The greatest protection of a bomber fleet against enemy fighter attack is very close formation, since protective firepower is concentrated. Wing tips of these large four-engine bombers were often as close as 10-30 feet from each other. As bomber fleets gained altitudes of 25,000 feet to 30,000 feet, fully loaded with bombs and residual fuel, formation flying became more difficult, since power settings were high and the air density low, causing flight control to be less responsive.

Flying in the rear of the formation in a "following" position makes close formation flying difficult, since position changes are magnified by the maneuvering of the forward aircraft. The tendency of the "following" aircraft in a large formation to become "loose" in compactness was always a problem. Often, this tendency became a matter of "life or death" in areas with enemy fighter aircraft present.

The sensation of flying close formation is wonderment that so many aircraft can be concentrated in such a small amount of airspace with few collisions. In World War II and the European theater of Operations (ETO), however, it became "business as usual"!

Lead

As First Pilots gained experience, Commanding Officers evaluated their performance for selection as prospective Lead Command Pilots. There was need for pilot skills and excellence in handling wingmen in formation flying. The quality of a complete Group formation of fifty-four (18x3) or thirty-six (12x3) aircraft was a measure of survival as well as pride.

Qualities that were important were smooth transitions in turns, let-downs, climbs, and expertise in recovery of the formation when aircraft losses occurred. When aircraft were damaged and out of formation, it seemed that enemy fighters were always waiting— German fighter "kill-rate" of crippled B-17G's was extremely high, and airmen's escape by parachute was very low.

Flying close meant wing tips on average were 50-80 feet from touching. The firepower of the B-17G's against fighter attack was critically more effective in close-formed formations. The German fighters knew this and usually attacked the loosely knit formations.

Another necessary aptitude was expertise at *short bomb runs* from the *initial point* (IP) when the bombardier zeros in on the target and bombs are released. A Norden bombsight was not used on every bombing B-17G. The responsibility of bomb release was the Lead Bombardier. Other bombardiers toggled their bomb loads for a bomb impact pattern achieving maximum damage. It was also important for the Lead Pilot to trim the aircraft and adjust the tricky autopilot for optimum flying with a Norden bombsight to assist the bombing execution.

The Lead Pilot had the responsibility after *bombs away* to exit the target area quickly and smoothly, and to form a close formation for expected probable fighter defense. Aircraft with heavy damage usually could not accelerate, perhaps not even hold altitude, so several left and right turns and slight drop in altitude allowed these and other aircraft to return to a tight formation. Cutting corners to fill the open spots in the formation was often essential to survival. This required ultimate aircrew discipline, as well as execution of appropriate maneuvers by the Lead Pilot.

There was a saying - *You bet your life on the skill of the Lead Pilot*!

In approaching anti-aircraft flak areas, Lead Command Pilots observed the flak patterns and varied the course to protect the formations. The greatest concentration of flak usually occurred near the IP and during the bomb-run. The shorter the bomb-run, the less flak damage and losses. However, target conditions influenced the amount of time necessary to seek and destroy the target.

If the bomb run failed to identify the target adequately, immediate decisions needed to be made by the Command Crew. Urgent consideration was then given to execution of a 360-degree turn and re-attack of the primary target or selection of a *"target of opportunity"* with a new IP and bomb-run. Discipline and execution of these protocols were important.

In Group Leads and 8th Air Force Leads, the Co-Pilot was also an Air Force Commander who stayed in touch with other Group formations. He reported strike times and results, and carried out other Command functions. The Lead Pilot carried out the flight decisions, bombing execution and maneuvers to control the formations. Both Pilot and Co-Pilot were trained in all Command functions in case of casualty to either one.

"B-17G Chin Turret"

The B-17 and Combat Tactics

The American (H) Heavy Bombardment aircraft in the European Theater of Operation (ETO) were the B-17 and the B-24, both 4-engine aircraft. By and large, the B-17 was assigned deep penetrations into central Germany, while the B-24 was used for other important missions. The B-17G had more defensive firepower against the *German Luftwaffe* fighter aircraft and seemed to be able to prolong flight after heavy battle damage. These points were often argued, but the B-17 was the dominant (H) Bomber in numbers and combat hours in the ETO.

The B-17E was the available heavy bomber at the outset of the heavy bombing missions in the ETO. The B-17F was introduced shortly thereafter. Combat experience pointed to a vulnerability of the B-17E and the B-17F to deadly Luftwaffe frontal fighter attacks. A modified B-17F. the B-17G, was delivered in early 1944. The B-17G had a nose "chin" turret which improved the survivability of the B-17 against enemy fighter frontal attacks. The B-17G had other improvements in armament and construction that were welcome to ETO aircrews, as well.

In the course of my tour of duty, I flew six new B-17G aircraft. One aircraft, however, was to provide a radar bombing capability in addition to visual bombing. As battle damage to the structure and engines made the aircraft unusable for air combat/bombing, it was retired. Frequently these battle-damaged aircraft were repaired for airworthiness and used for utility and training; sometimes they were used for salvage and parts that were always needed.

It is interesting to note that the Luftwaffe tactics dramatically changed after the introduction of the B-17G. In the beginning, the Luftwaffe would swarm the Lead B-17E and B-17F aircraft from a *12 o'clock high* position. This resulted in a large loss of Command Lead aircraft, which, obviously, interacted with bombing operations.

As the B-17G's became more available, the Luftwaffe changed its combat stratagems to attacks on B-17G's from the side and rear of the formation. FW-190 generally attacked from *9 o'clock low*. The ME-109's had 20mm cannons that they preferred to fire through a formation from the rear, since a miss on the first target might hit the aircraft in front. As a consequence, ME-109 attacks generally came from *6 o'clock* positions.

A few extra seconds of firepower from the B-17G often was the difference between "life and death" for the aircrew. Experience and study of enemy fighter tactics were absolutely critical elements for survival of bombing formations.

American fighter protection was outstanding. All bomber aircrews appreciated and revered the superior efforts of our *Little Friends* and held them in the highest esteem. As American fighter aircraft became more available in mid-to-late 1944 for assignment to *ramrod* (bomber protection), the Luftwaffe adopted *"hit and run"* tactics. Usually it meant a quick pass from *high* positions with a rapid low exit to escape from B-17G 50-caliber gun ranges.

The B-17 was a wonderful aircraft in its time. The aircrews were forever diligent in survival schemes. Some schemes worked and some didn't, but every little bit of knowledge and preparation helped survival.

Lead Pilot Commanders studied flak concentrations and enemy fighter tactics continuously. It was important to study reports of flak concentrations to avoid being surprised. Routes that minimized routes over known flak areas were critical for survival. If flak was encountered, it was important to watch the patterns and the tracking. It was also important to keep communication channels clear to warn following formations of problems.

As the formations entered likely areas of heavy anti-aircraft defenses, the courses were varied left and right every minutes or so to minimize accurate enemy tracking——just a few degrees each way seemed to complicate the enemy anti-aircraft tracking process. Flak barrages were devastating. If a barrage couldn't be completely avoided, it was important to skirt the flak barrage area as much as possible. On a bomb run, after the "IP" had been reached, the course was invariably set. It was essential to make the duration on the final bomb-run as brief as possible. After *"bombs away, i*t was critical to escape the target area quickly and recover with a close formation. It required extreme skill to accomplish these maneuvers well.

The lessons learned in air combat suggest that survival was related to detail planning and expert execution, but most of all—*God Willing*.

Practice Practice Practice

It may seem strange to read about the constant practice and training as we became seasoned veterans. It was obviously appropriate for new replacement aircrews, but it might seem a paradox for experienced aircrews that supposedly had combat skills well in hand. It was particularly important for Lead aircrews, since perfection meant successful missions and a higher probability of survival for the entire Group.

Practice and training was a between-mission exercise that included live gunnery, quick target sighting and practice bomb delivery, navigational target improvisations, and upgrading pilot skills.

There was extreme emphasis on close formation flying. The key to close formation flying was practice of both the "leaders" and "the led". Practice made close formation flying more routine and comfortable—much less tiring on our long missions. Formation leaders practiced smooth maneuvers, while holding altitude to prevent "spreading" a formation. Executing practice flak evasion maneuvers made formation leaders more conscious of the limits of their flight changes to keep their formations intact. Assembling a scattered formation into a close formation required practice of both Lead Pilots and other aircrew pilots—what to do, what to expect, and how to do it. Lead Pilots needed to practice turning a formation on the I.P. and to execute a short bomb run (less than 60 seconds). Bombardiers needed quick resolution of their targeting and practiced accordingly. A short bomb run, as previously mentioned, reduced battle damage and increased aircrew survival.

As tired as I often was, I routinely practiced between missions. In the final analysis, it was a major contributor to my survival and the survival of those I led into combat.

Is This Combat

Returning from a 48-hour leave, I learned that I had been assigned to new quarters in the 324ᵗʰ Bomb Squadron Command Pilothouse. This was an unexpected surprise, but a welcome one, since it was a large residence-type home with facilities that one would hardly associate with War and combat conditions. It featured a bath with hot water, private rooms with a fireplace in each room, an orderly to maintain the premises, a back yard with a high wooden fence about it, and even a garage for jeeps and bicycles. It was wonderful!

As I returned to the realities of combat preparation, our next two days were filled with a full curriculum of ground school, practice bombing, practice formation and link trainer. We were busy!

Food about this time of year was good, but we were growing tired of cold cuts, powdered eggs, Spam, and Brussel sprouts. We had also located a black-market egg dealer who was willing to do us a favor at a price of approximately 20 cents per egg. Eggs were at a premium—we had no complaints!

A new group of replacement crews arrived to supplement our diminished Squadron. As we looked at the crew lists within our Squadron, I was now among the high-mission crews with six accredited missions. It seemed strange and paradoxical to mention a high-mission crew and six missions in the same breath. There it was however, boldly exhibited where all could see, on the crew-list blackboard attached to the operation office wall.

So far my crew was without serious casualties and reasonably well adjusted to the Base. Food was good; quarters were excellent and we were proud of our Squadron. Yes, Bassingbourn was a comfortable home in England, considering the limitations and problems of an active War.

Home of the Doodle-Bug

The *Buzz Bomb* is now committed to World War II history, but in mid-summer 1944 it was a reality. London and other areas in England were feeling the concussion of the ingenious robot bomb, the Buzz Bomb – a pilotless, jet-propelled bomb with wings and 1000 pounds of destruction. When I think of the Buzz Bomb, which the English called unaffectionately the *Doodle-Bug*, I think of its terrorizing, deafening, staccato roar, the hesitation as the engine cuts out, the long seconds of fearful silence, then the detonation. It was hard on morale! The demoralizing aspect of these robot bombs was that there was no way of knowing where they would hit next. Its target was an indiscriminate one.

Near Berlin to the north and west, on the shores of the North Sea, intelligence reports revealed the existence of a laboratory. This was the laboratory in which the Buzz Bomb was conceived and born, and out of which it had grown to menace even non-combatant children and women in their homes. We could only guess what might be a test-tube baby today, and a full-grown menacing monster tomorrow. The laboratory had to go—it had to be completely and utterly destroyed. On the morning of the 18th of July 1944, we were on our way across the English Channel with just this proposal in mind. Our target was Peenemunde, Germany —our aiming point, the center of the laboratory buildings.

We approached the target from the northeast; visibility and weather were excellent for bombing. The first Groups over the target were carrying 1000-pound concrete-piercing bombs—the following Groups, incendiary bombs. The first bombs were to reduce the buildings to rubble; the subsequent incendiary bombs were to fire, burn, and "gut" what was left.

Flak was not extremely intense, but it was accurate. We were hit badly twice before *"bombs away"*, but managed to hold formation. A low burst on the starboard side perforated our outboard main gasoline tank, but no explosion occurred. The starboard #4 engine was also damaged. We learned upon landing that our main wing-spar was partially shot away, requiring a complete new installation. A second burst—a flak explosion— was low under the B-17G nose. The right foot of our Navigator was injured slightly and the forward B-17G "greenhouse" was shattered, also taking out part of my instrument panel. The majority of my instruments were unusable. This burst took out the hydraulic system as well. Although hits were scored in other sections of the aircraft, the main damage was inflicted by these two flak bursts.

We dropped our bombs with success and continued to hold formation relatively well. I directed the Bombardier to render first aid to the Navigator and lift him up to the Pilot's cabin, but the task was completed efficiently even as I spoke into the intercom. I was then advised of the seriousness of our first casualty.

We limped home with no further incident. A *red-red flare* was fired as we approached for landing to indicate to those on the ground we had injured personnel aboard and we had serious battle damage.

Our brakes, normally operated hydraulically, were inoperative, so we improvised a method to slow the B-17G after "touch down" in the landing. The method involved merely attaching parachutes to the tail spar, the waist gun mounts, and the brace in the radio room. As we "touched down" on the runway, the parachutes were to be released, and theoretically the plane should be slowed down. Although this method was used subsequently with success, our first trial was a disappointment. The parachutes collapsed and were of no practical use after that. We had another alternative in mind—we successfully "ground-looped" and "belly-landed" the aircraft at the end of the runway as it slowed in the landing run. We came to a sudden stop, and, shortly thereafter, an ambulance removed the injured Navigator, and a staff car raced from the Base control tower to investigate the situation.

We destroyed Peenemunde, Germany, that day, and were assured that Doodlebug production was at an end. London would be pleased about that, for Doodlebugs were terrorizing as they randomly destroyed property and civilians.

In late summer 1944, there were huge explosions scattered randomly around London. It was later discovered that Peenemunde had developed a "V-2" rocket propelled by a liquid-fuel rocket motor. Its payload was a highly destructive 2000-pound bomb. The successful heavy bomber mission to Peenemunde also destroyed a major German capability to engineer and develop these large ballistic rockets.

Mission 7 was "in the books"!

<u>**"B-17G Blown Nose"**</u>

Target Germany

We were scarcely in bed before orderlies were waking us for our next mission—Mission 8. Strangely, I was the only member of my original crew alerted, and I was perplexed at this sudden turn of events. I had been assigned to Group Lead Pilot, with 54 B-17G's in my formation, and with this assignment, aircrews were shifted. I learned now that my original crew was to be replaced with a more experienced one. Not one of the other nine constituent members in our original unit had flown in a *Flying Fortress* with anyone else except me at the controls, so the reorganization affected our feelings deeply.

Although the promotion to a more responsible position was noteworthy, I fought my new crew assignment. As happens so often, ours was not the choice; my original crew was reassigned to my Co-pilot, who was promoted to First Pilot.

My former aircrew was as disappointed over this reassignment as I was—we had grown attached through the trials of the previous months. We had supreme confidence in our ability as a unit to weather any situation, whatever it might be. We were all happy, however, on the co-pilot's promotion. I was advised that the reassignment was final, and it was time to move on.

Our next target was near Augsburg in southern Germany. Our "aiming point" was the center of the hanger area on a German airfield, called *Lechfeld*. Intelligence had reported activity on a novel jet-propelled, aircraft, the ME-262, which we were to meet later. The mission instructions, "Installations are to be destroyed."

The early part of the mission was uneventful as we skirted the Swiss Alps, although radio reports informed us that formations to our rear were under sustained enemy fighter attack.

I particularly remember this mission to Lechfeld, Germany, since two of my friends, flying in another Squadron attached to the 91st Bomb Group, were lost on this day. Lts. Braund and Burwick collided, flying in the rear of the formation as flak bursts seemed momentarily to center about their unit. Observers were in disagreement on what actually precipitated the collision. It seemed that Lt. Burwick's aircraft momentarily rose, drew ahead, then faltered and dropped down on the plane piloted by Lt. Braund, ripping the wings and tearing two engines from each aircraft as the collision occurred. Both aircraft immediately started spinning, and our last view, 10,000 feet below us, showed the planes still spinning out of control. No parachutes were observed to leave either aircraft, so all crewmembers were presumed lost.

We turned for the target, approaching from the south. In the distance to the east, we observed a flak cloud over Munich as a deploying Force feinted at the city to draw enemy attention from our actual target. Flak became more intense as our target was sighted. In front of us, German anti-aircraft scored a direct hit on a B-17G either in the Bomb-bay, or in a gasoline tank. The Flying Fortress became a flaming orange and black ball of pyrotechnics. Seconds later there was a terrific explosion as the plane disintegrated. Pieces rebounded off our windshield and the body of our aircraft. We sustained damage, but could not determine the immediate danger to our aircraft. Apparently no vital mechanisms were damaged.

We turned on the IP. After a 45 second bomb run, bombs dropped away, and fell "true". Photographs showed a tremendous explosion in the hangers as our bombs dropped in the proverbial *pickle barrel*. Barrage-type heavy anti-aircraft flak over the target could not be avoided—damage was heavy, but no B-17G's were lost.

Lechfeld was destroyed, but we had paid a heavy price. It was estimated that over 80% of the aircraft attacking the target in our formation incurred battle damage. The ground crews would be busy into the night repairing and replacing parts of our B-17G's after we touched down from this trip.

As I landed and parked on the hardstand, all my boys, the crewmembers of my original crew, were out to see if all was right. They had *sweated* me in, waiting for my safe return.

The patient waiting and anticipation of combat aircrews returning from a mission was an awesome experience. The ground crews and compatriot pilots not on the mission would gather at spots around the control tower, usually in small groups. Information from the control tower would be relayed to the gathering. As the expected arrival time approached, the tension mounted.

As the first B-17G's arrived, the *counting* began as the aircraft circled the field once to allow damaged planes and those with injured crewmen to land first. *Red-Red flares* always were fired on the first approach to indicate that priority. Ambulances and fire-fighting groups were then prepared for these troubled aircraft.

The ID numbers on the returning B-17G's were observed by binoculars and called out as they passed. The missing B-17G's, the red-red flares, and obvious battle damage on the B-17G's brought high anxiety and worry. The dreadful feelings, as losses were identified as friends, caused sorrow-filled reactions.

As the final B-17G landed and taxied to it's station, the ground crews for each returning aircraft raced in their jeeps to greet the aircrews; some crews very sadly realized their stations would be empty for this day.

In the Squadrons, the blackboard listing of crews and aircraft were adjusted by simply erasing the entry. It never changed—it was the concluding action each mission.

Mission 8 was complete.

Two More

The following morning on the 20th of July 1944, our target was Leipzig, Germany, a munitions depot. Our route was more direct than usual and bombing altitude increased to 27,000 feet. Weather enroute was excellent until we neared the target, where low clouds obscured the enemy munitions depot. Under the existing target circumstances, we directed our bombing to an alternate target - a railway yard filled with war materiel. Our bombing was considered destructive, but maximum damage was not inflicted. Flak was modest at the target, and the formations incurred very little flak battle damage. Strangely, the greatest damage to our formation occurred on the return route. The Lead Navigator miscalculated our position, and we found ourselves suddenly over an apparently important enemy installation. Anti-aircraft fire flared suddenly, and the sky seemed to blacken. For approximately 4 minutes we maneuvered the formation, twisted *within* the formation, and tried to break free from accurate German gunnery. The flak ceased almost as suddenly as it started, as we passed out of range. 15 B-17G's, however, incurred heavy battle damage. Three additional aircraft were critically damaged; all three never returned to England. Close friends, Lt. Bare and Capt. Holmes, piloted two of these aircraft. It seemed that my coterie of friends grew smaller and smaller with each mission. The death toll mounted!

We had accumulated three consecutive missions on the 18th, 19th and 20th of July, 1944. If an airman or an aircrew was grounded for flying fatigue, our expression was that he was *"flying fat"*. We were scheduled to "fly fat" for the next 48 hours. On the anniversary of my first month in combat on July 20, 1944, I had accumulated 9 missions.

This ninth mission, however, was my first major combat injury. While not critical, it caused a stir.

As I left my pilot's seat, I noticed a sticky feeling as I rose. My pilot's seat was red with blood. My co-pilot noticed it, and said loudly, "Your butt is soaked with blood!" I didn't seem disabled so I decided to check it out myself before getting the medics involved. We sometimes avoided the medics because they had the authority to "ground you" from flying for longer periods than desired.

I stopped in Squadron Headquarters on the way to debriefing. I had been hit in the butt by a piece of German irregular shrapnel about the size of a very small olive, and it could be visually seen. The Orderly took some surgical tweezers and removed the shrapnel easily. After the Orderly cleaned the shallow wound, powdered the wound with the famous "sulfa" medication, and applied a pressure bandage, I proceeded to debriefing. Very little was said about it at the time, but all pilots often have a chatty Co-pilot.

Of course, it became known! My crew chief fitted a section of armor plate on my pilots seat (Co-pilot's seat, too), and left a note, "Sir, you now have an iron ass"! Of course, the title of "Iron Ass" resulted. It might have been appropriate, since I was "heavy" on flight discipline in my mission Leads. I healed quickly and missed no missions.

48 Hour Leave

As I recall, my leisure time was usually spent in London. Since I was away from home I appreciated the small things, those many small things that ordinarily escape us when we refuse to take the time to enjoy the spare moments. It might be only an American movie, or a comfortable bed, or perhaps even having food served in a "genteel" manner. What gilded a sojourn in London escapes me, but I did enjoy my leave time spent there. On this 48 hour leave I was determined to see *London Town*, for talk and rumor was spreading throughout the military units that London was soon to be declared "off limits", a prohibited area, since *"Buzz Bombs"* recently had killed and injured a number of visiting American airmen.

For ten shillings, the American equivalent of two dollars, I commandeered one of those old-fashioned taxis to tour London Town. I visited St. Paul's Cathedral, the Tower of London, Buckingham Palace, Parliament, the Thames River, Fleet Street, the Strand, Piccadilly Circus, the Wax Museum, Trafalgar Square, the blitz section of London, London Bridge, and, above all, Westminster Abbey. As I looked upon the reverent grandeur of this aged structure, I could not, and do not wish here to attempt to describe the feelings that were so inspiring. Someday in the future, I anticipate revisiting my old friend, for I seldom missed paying a call to Westminster Abbey on my trips to London. I often strolled along the Thames River on early mornings, watching the riverboats. The gardens behind the Savoy

Hotel facing the river were also a favorite spot. I always found my way to the Strand Palace Hotel Grill for luncheon, where I often ordered a glass of English lager, cold lobster salad, and apple flan—(not exactly, a War diet). The stringed orchestra accompanied the luncheon with a repertoire of famous music from the past and present.

It was usually Grovenor House, Gennaro's, the Italian Club, or Claridge's for dinner, with a good stage play in one of the many London theaters afterwards.

There were times when I visited the poorer sections of London and met the English commoner. One old gentleman invited me "to tea" on one of these excursions, "Yank," he offered, "Will you do me the honor of having a spot of tea?"

I accepted, because he genuinely seemed to mean it. We had tea and pastries. While brimming with pride, he spoke of his son in France and the job he was doing in the War. His other son was lost at Dunkerque. He spoke earnestly and was proud of both sons.

I enjoyed London on my visits. Some day I hope to return under less auspicious circumstances to see London in peacetime.

An Accounting

While in London this last time, "on leave", I ran upon one of my classmates at the Savoy Hotel American Bar. We lingered over a glass of lager and recalled experiences, old and new. There had been about thirty-five of us in the beginning; there were less than that now – the toll was mounting. Already, of those we knew about, Lt.O'Bannon was lost on the mission to Berlin; Lts. Braund and Burwick, at Lechfeld; Lts. Bare and Beaudry and Captain Holmes, at Leipzig; Lt. Pridwell, on the enemy coast; Lts. Arce, Bunker, Assell, and Hamilton were known dead as well. Within scarcely ten missions our group had been decimated.

We left the American Bar remembering how our rationalization always repeated itself in our minds, "It's bound to happen to some of us, but it won't happen to me!" It seemed to be a feeling of invincibility. Later we wondered!

Troop Support

Progress in France after our invasion landings had "bogged down"-—the going was rough, so the *Doughfoot* (muddy-booted American Infantry Man) called upon their flying brothers to lend a helping hand.

We were briefed on the morning of the 24th of July, 1944 for troop support at St. Lo, France, where the Germans were strongly resisting our inland advance. Our instructions were to fly over our troops and lay a carpet of small, shrapnel-type, anti-personnel bombs over an area where reconnaissance had reported the enemy in strength.

Inasmuch as reports of anti-air defenses were not heavy and accurate bombing was a necessity, we were to fly at 12000 feet for bombing. Each unit had a specific aiming point to sow a pattern of death on the German-held French landscape, so that no German would escape the debacle alive.

The mission was scheduled for late morning. We were barely in formation before our bomb-bays were opening for the bomb run. Since the approach was over our own troops, no anti-aircraft fire evasion was expected. For the same reason, however, our bomb-bays were opened early over the English Channel. It was not an unusual occurrence for the entire bomb load to release when the bomb-bay opened, due to malfunctions in the electrical system that energized the whole unit, or bomb racks.

Seconds before "bombs away", our target was suddenly blocked "from sight" by smoke and poor visibility. We received an urgent emergency call *to "hold bombs"*. The proper code authorization message satisfied us that the message was reliable. We returned to Bassingbourn without dropping a single bomb. The cargo of anti-personnel bombs were still loaded in tiers in our Bomb-bay which meant that our landing had to be "delicate" or we had to disgorge the bombs in the English Channel. We landed safely.

Bombs had dropped from several other formations and questionable damage had been inflicted. Some of that damage was to our own troops—the sighting was poor and the bombs fell far short of their intended target. We spoke of the mission later as *"one of those things"—mistakes* that happen!Our own troop support effort had gone amiss this once, but "no damage", and we were to have an opportunity to prove our value in troop support at a later date.

Battle Damage

Battle damage to the B-17G's was a constant worry for both the operating aircrews and the ground crews that maintained the aircraft. The B-17G was unusually durable and could remain airborne with the loss of as many as two engines, as well as large surface damage on the fuselage and wings. The B-17G also remained airborne with structural damage to large sections of the aircraft, such as nose, wings, and tail areas. The primary causes of battle damage were Luftwaffe fighter attacks and anti-aircraft flak hits.

The Me-109E featured 20 mm cannon and the FW-190 had fixed machine guns. Both fighters were fearsome, since their attacks were frequently pointed at the wing fuel tanks and the bomb-filled bomb-bay at the center of the fuselage—a hit meant an explosion and complete destruction of the B-17G. It was 20 mm cannons that missed critical areas that left gaping holes about the aircraft. Machine guns often destroyed sections of the B-17G elevators, rudder, or wing area, if the attack was not totally destructive.

Examples of B-17G severe battle damage are shown in Illustrations that follow.

Anti-aircraft flak defenses "tracked" formations and attempted to achieve direct hits on B-17G's. while achieving collateral damage in the process. In heavily-defended areas, the German defense strategy was to establish a dense flak barrier—any aircraft penetrating the barrier would have battle damage.

Flak manifested itself in black cloud puffs that seemed innocuous in appearance, but hundreds of small metal particles (shrapnel) would exit from this black cloud puff to damage B-17G aircraft. At altitudes of 25,000 feet, or more, the effective range of this flak was estimated to be 50-100 yards. Density of German anti-aircraft batteries was estimated to range from 10-1,000 guns, depending on the target. A major oil refinery (Merseburg) or ball-bearing factory (Schweinfurt) were among the most heavily defended industrial targets. Heavy battle damage could always be predicted in these heavily defended areas, and both ground crews and aircrews dreaded a target assignment anywhere near them. Not all the flak would impact critical aircraft equipment, or aircrew, or structure, but the probabilities caused concern.

As protective equipment, the aircrew wore flak vests and flak helmets to prevent injury from random-flying pieces of flak. On one occasion, the ground crew counted over 500 holes from flak in my B-17G pilot/co-pilot/engineer flight cabin location.

Oil and Flak

Of all the targets in Germany, one of the most prized and heavily defended installations of all was the huge mile-long fuel refinery a few miles west of Leipzig, Germany, at Merseburg. Our losses were usually extreme on this mission because, almost without exception, it attracted notable fighter opposition and heavy, intense anti-aircraft fire. Although we had crippled the refinery and destroyed sections of the complex in prior missions, the installation had never been completely decommissioned. The installation was difficult to destroy since it was over a mile long and narrowly "strung-out" along a river. It required almost direct hits to destroy its refining capability.

German armies, particularly their tanks and efficient motorized units in France, were desperate for fuel and oil supplies. The Luftwaffe had been handicapped by our destructive air raids and air combat several months before. In May and early June 1944, many of our targets were small fuel depots and small refineries. By late July 1944, the Germans were feeling the results of our missions. German equipment was being deserted on the battlefield for lack of fuel and supplies "to make it run".

On the 28th of July 1944, we were briefed for Merseburg, Germany, with our "aiming point" the power supply unit and the nearby distillation towers narrowly located near the river. The bombing results on Merseburg were mixed – again, target damage, but not large destruction. The high bombing altitude, high lateral winds, accurate and heavy anti-aircraft flak, and enemy fighter opposition always was a deterrent to our bombing efforts.

Although my close formations were not attacked, enemy fighters ahead and to our rear decimated other B-17G' formations before air support could reach them.

I remember the heavy flak and the resultant damage—five *B-17G's* from my formation were lost over the target. Although we were hit again and again, we made the return trip without further incident.

We required an engine change, two gasoline tanks removed and replaced, and repairs for heavy *skin* damage (the metal covering the plane is called *skin*). We counted over 150 holes in the aircraft and were fortunate to escape crew injuries under the circumstances. Flak suits saved many. For example, one large piece of flak pierced the nose Plexiglas striking the Bombardier in the chest—the flak suit saved his life.

Others, however, suffered aircrew casualties. Lt. Collins, for example, found his Radio Operator as if asleep with his head on the table in front of him. He was dead. A small piece of flak no larger than a penny had slipped between the flak suit pads to enter his side and pierce vital organs. The body was removed, and Lt. Collins sat up late that night writing a letter --one of those letters that never seem to be adequate, but a letter that might partially offer solace his family. As soon as the War Department notified the next of kin, the letter would be forwarded.

For two days following, we were grounded for repairs to the aircraft in the Merseburg mission. Battle damage of major-repair nature was estimated at 70%—7 out of 10 aircraft were unable to fly the following day after the mission.

WE LOATHED MERSEBURG!

We were in the beginning of a psychological transformation. In addition to the psychological problems associated with the immediate task of *"doing a job"* was added a hateful feeling for those who precipitated a selfish war where civilian men, women, and children were hurt. Although at times we tendered doubts about fighting thousands of miles from our homes and families,somewhere, during the tour of combat duty most of us changed our perspective of WWII.

A Return Visit

As soon as a sufficient number of B-17G's were flyable, we were alerted for a return visit to Munich on the 31st of July, 1944. On the outskirts of Munich, a large industrial plant, although damaged, was still operating. Our target and objective was "to destroy the factory installation completely".

Enemy fighters did not engage us, and the flak was noticeably weaker than usual. We destroyed the installation with bombs placed directly on the target. We returned with no losses and small battle damage, and we noted that "the ground crews will be happy about that, after Merseburg"!

Weather was reasonably good, but I remember my heated-suit unit malfunctioned. At 50 F degrees below zero, I was uncomfortable the last part of the mission. I felt measurably better when we descended to lower altitudes and higher temperatures. I did not require treatment for frostbite—the plague of high-altitude flying, where the skin breaks and gains a transparency that resembles a ripe tomato that has been frozen solid and allowed to thaw. Exposure and frostbite were painful injuries.

This mission was non-incidental for the most part, though long and trying. This was among the last missions to Munich, Germany. Effectively, Munich was written off as an 8th Air Force strategic target.

Foxholes in the Sky

From the beginning, the tail gunner of my original aircrew carried a doorknob on each and every combat mission he flew. This doorknob was as much a part of his equipment as the oxygen mask he used at altitude in more rare atmospheres. The function of the doorknob was an enigma, but he was inseparable from his "lucky-piece".

Actually, he was hardly different from most of us. It did'nt seem to make the least bit of difference whether it was a doorknob, a Bible, a rabbit's foot, a wife's handkerchief, or a pair of baby's shoes. In one way or another, we all inherently had our little superstitions.

Superstition expressed itself in aversion to renaming an aircraft after one that had been shot down. Some combat aircrews refused to fly in any aircraft with the word, *flak*, or any association with *flak* incorporated in the name of the plane. There were, of course, always the *unlucky* planes in every Squadron. It may sound childish and strange to many, but the facts of the case are true.

I think in most of us, deep within us, is a fear for the unknown—that quantity that we can't explain or rationalize. When the answers are vague and uncertain, when "life and death" decisions are an everyday occurrence, we revert sometimes to strange thinking, but all in all basic convictions will prevail. Religion cannot be denied a place in war. Religion is very much a part of each individual, and individuals make up the Armies that fight the war. A byword in modern war terminology is that *"there is no such thing as an atheist in a foxhole"*. This statement finds an extension into airmen's cockpits, so to speak—in *"foxholes in the sky"*. It was difficult to explain and rationalize many of the catastrophes, the lucky-pieces, the aversions, our little superstitions, but it is part of the mental work of playing the serious game of war.

Results Too Excellent

Enemy aircraft based near the front lines continually harassed and aggravated the progress of our Armies on the Normandy Front. On the morning of the 1st of August 1944, we were to destroy a German-occupied airfield at Chartres, France.

Mission 13 was carried out with excellent results. Our bombings destroyed runways, hangers and storage installations for further immediate use. As our Armies swept over France and the airfield at Chartres was captured, it was a long and arduous task to reconstruct the installation for our own use. In a way, perhaps the bombing job was too well done.

Though the flak was not intense, again it was extremely accurate. The flak damage in our immediate formation was light, but the other two formations suffered three direct hits with all three aircraft crashing. Lt. "Tex" Thompson, a good friend throughout the past few months, suffered a direct burst amidships, which broke his aircraft in half. A parachute-less body disengaged from the tail section to plummet to earth, while another body dangled from the tail section when the parachute fouled on the vertical stabilizer. No parachutes were reported seen from the front half of the B-17G. None of the occupants of the three downed aircraft were ever heard from again. It was a tragic ending for Lt. Thompson and his crew. I remember the tail section floating down through the air like a leaf—it would glide, then dive and spin a little, then glide again in a wide circle, and finally several pieces broke off and it plummeted earthward.

Mission 13 completed!

Post Mission Debriefing

An important part of a mission was to provide data after its completion. A mission was far from completed after landing at the home Base. Following transit from our aircraft to the equipment rooms, we were usually offered coke or a small glass of brandy to unwind and were then interrogated by experienced Intelligence and Operations and USAF Command personnel.

A debriefing usually started with an overview of the mission, explaining irregularities, target damage, anti-aircraft locations, enemy fighter identification and tactics. Identification and observations of lost aircraft, the number of parachutes (if any) that exited an aircraft and conditions of the returning B-17G's's were among the other subjects. Interrogations lasted usually 20-45 minutes—then "off" for a shower and our own private psychological repair.

If there were losses in my formation, I immediately, within 24 hours, wrote a letter to the family. These were difficult letters about a grief-stricken subject—the loss of a loved one. Usually the Squadron Commanding Officer also penned his anguished regrets on behalf of the Squadron.

There were a lot of letters!

Little Friends

Two days later, on the 3rd of August 1944, we were back to Germany again, with our target a railway junction at Mulhause, Germany. Supplies and railway equipment had collected to supply the German Forces in the south of France. On this mission the 91st bomb Group led the entire 8th Air Force, a bombing Force of approximately 800 aircraft.

The outstanding feature of this mission was not flak, or enemy fighter attacks, or aircraft lost, but rather the excellent fighter cover provided us by our *Little Friends*. Weaving back and forth, sometimes practically in our formation, the little American P-51 *Mustang* fighters hovered about us. We had little fear of any enemy fighter action this day, which was a reassuring fact to us all.

Two of the three formations that comprised our 91st Bomb Group bombed Mulhause, with results unobserved due to a broken cloud structure below us. The third formation bombed a German airfield with excellent results observed.

No aircraft were lost and very light damage was incurred from light anti-aircraft action. We returned to Bassingborne without incident.

Mission 14 Complete

Sitting Target

The British near Caen, France, were experiencing difficulty advancing against a strong German Force, so the American heavy bombers were briefed to support the British troops in the SW Bretteville-Sur Laize, France, area on the 8th of August, 1944. To guarantee accurate bombing, this mission was a low-level raid flown at 11,000 feet. With the memory of the tragic circumstances of our St.Lo mission still fresh in our minds, extreme emphasis was made that no bomb was to be released until the "aiming point" was positively identified. We were among the last of the Bomb Groups to fly over the target. By the time we were sighted on the target, smoke and dust from the preceding units obscured our aiming point. We, consequently, released no bombs from our formation

The friendly-occupied area at this time in early August was still relatively small, and the heavy bombers soon congested the air space above the British troops. Whereas we were briefed to fly over enemy territory for only a few short minutes, the progression of events gradually altered our route. The bomber stream slowly edged south till we were over enemy installations.

Heavy head winds slowed our speed over the ground. As well, British artillery was not coordinated to eliminate the enemy anti-aircraft fire. The accumulation of all these events prefaced a disastrous situation, for at 11,000 feet, enemy anti-aircraft fire is extremely accurate. Each burst of flak seemed to pick a bomber from the sky—I never saw so many direct hits. Even the sounds of the flak bursts were audible, which was new to us, for at higher altitudes, no sound is heard.

All formations suffered heavy crew casualties. I remember vividly one Flying Fortress scarcely more than 100 yards ahead of us suddenly disintegrating with a blinding orange and black flash. Our B-17G was covered with oil, and pieces of flying metal scored our wings and fuselage.

This mission marked our next-to-last "low-level" heavy bombing mission. The 91st Bomb Group filled thirteen ambulances with casualties on our return—the hospitals were congested with aircrews. The 8th Air Force had been hard hit on a seemingly easy mission—responsibility was given to low-altitude operations, the failure of the British to neutralize the enemy anti-aircraft positions, the congestion in the area, and the poor navigational route.

Regardless of the explanation, we suffered heavily on the target that we scarcely considered more than a *milk-run*.

Mission 15 Complete

Between Missions

Aircrews were closely-knit units, as most combat units. It was a practice to visit the Base Hospital several miles away to see aircrew that had been wounded. The quality of medical service and nursing attention were absolutely outstanding. The Hospital Staff was very cooperative and invited our visits. As a result we often got acquainted in a casual way.

In late 1944, the 324th Bomb Squadron had a number of our aircrew in the Base Hospital. Among those was one of my top engineer-turret gunners, Sgt. McCall, who was undergoing non-critical, but painful surgery. A particularly attractive First Lieutenant nurse was responsible for his ward and his care. Lt. Cindy Strong and her pleasant manner also made my visits more frequent. Sgt. McCall said to me during a visit, "I put some great words together about you, Lieutenant, and she seemed interested. Why don't you ask Lt. Strong to have dinner with you?"

It was a Base Hospital policy that medical personnel stay emotionally uninvolved with combat aircrews for professional and other reasons, but there were gross defections from this policy. While dating existed and partying occurred from time to time, it didn't "*square*" with War activities that required "secrecy", 7-day work schedules, and the grueling demands of flying air combat.

Lt. Strong, off Base called Cindy, accepted my invitation, and we had a wonderful time. She later invited me to the Base Hospital Officers' Club for dinner—and so it went!

I learned that she had previously known an aircrew Navigator. After several months, the Navigator was killed in air combat. It was a devastating experience for her, and she still felt the effect of his untimely death. It was an honest confession of a personal nature, and I admired her for being "open" about it, and told her so. We continued our dinner routines for several weeks during which I had two missions. Sgt. McCall informed me that during the missions that I was flying, she was beside herself until the Base informed her that I had returned safely. I was only halfway through my missions, and I visualized this as a serious problem if we continued to see each other. We discussed the matter further. She was transferred several days later. We hoped to see each other after the War was over, but it didn't happen, which in itself is sad.

Another interlude in my social activities included a London date with a strange beginning. The Royal Air Force (RAF) had several bistros in London where RAF flyers congregated for social activities. I had trained in basic flying with the RAF in Lancaster, California, so I felt I was entitled to entry in one Club in particular. The Club admitted me graciously, and I was seated alone at a small table adjoining a foursome of two RAF pilots and two very pretty girls. When the RAF pilots left the table to greet several of their flying friends, I visited briefly with one of the pretty girls, a little, shapely blond lady. While the conversation was brief, since the RAF pilots were away only a few minutes, it was obvious the young lady and I liked each other. The RAF pilots on their return were upset and made uncomplimentary remarks about Americans in general and American pilots in particular. I had very little to say, but it finally came to the point that they invited me "to leave" the bistro. In the meantime, I wrote a note on a slip of paper, "I will meet you in 20 minutes outside, in front of the bar, in a taxi with the motor running." It was too unpleasant to remain longer, so I left. As I left, I slipped the note to her. In about 25-30 minutes she came out, and we were "away" for dinner and a wonderful evening. She was lovely, apparently from a distinguished family, and absolutely charming.

This was our only date. By the time I was able to get my next leave to London, her family had sent her on a *holiday* outside England and the War. I had hoped she would respond to my letters, but I'm not sure she ever received them.

Ostheim, Goslar, A Promotion, and a Barrel

On the 15th of August 1944, we bombed an enemy airfield at Ostheim, Germany with excellent results. Losses were light, and the flak damage negligible. All aircraft returned without incident.

Personnel Orders were received in the Squadron promoting me to 1st Lieutenant. With several of the other promoted Officers, I bought a barrel of lager for the Officers' Club. We gathered that night to celebrate, but ended reminiscing as usual.

On the 24th of August 1944, our briefed target was Goslar, Germany, an important airfield in the vicinity of Leipzig, Germany. The mission was uneventful until we neared the IP. German anti-aircraft batteries were "tracking" the Lead Command B-17G uncomfortably close as we made flak evasive maneuvers. We turned on the IP, hoping the turn on the IP would disturb the close anti-aircraft "tracking". Flak evasive maneuvers were now restricted, since we were on the bomb run. Suddenly, a heavy flak burst hit in front and near the "Lead" Command B-17G on the starboard side. The flak explosion caused slight structural wing damage, loss of the #4 outboard engine, and the # 3 engine was smoking. Increasing the dilemma, the bomb load would not "release" for unknown reasons. With a full bomb load, loss of an engine and another engine feathered, we immediately started losing altitude.

I advised the Deputy Commander to "take over" while making a second attempt to unload our bombs. The bombs still would not "release". The formation, however, remained intact in close formation with the Deputy Commander in charge.

The thought occurred to me, in those moments, that we had survived a dozen, or so, hard and difficult missions, and we were "on our way" to finalizing our tour of duty. Why now! Why should we be "going down" on a comparatively easy mission?

Anyway! Enough! "Get a target" and survive!

Our secondary target was a short distance from our primary target, so we decided to make a try for it, in spite of our inability to hold our normal 25,000 foot bombing altitude. Rapid calculations by the Bombardier, coordination in the cockpit, and an alternate method of "releasing" the bombs was devised. As we were *"going down"* over Germany, we "released" our bombs at 20,000 feet and scored a "direct hit". The results were excellent and visually observed.

Our rate of loss of altitude decreased, although we had already lost 5,000 feet. We were now barely able to hold altitude at 20,000 feet. The formation stayed with us, however. Enemy fighters were in the area, as they usually were whenever we approached the environs of Leipzig, Germany. We called our "Little Friends" for fighter cover, and they responded.

We were unable to maintain contact through regular radio channels, so the Deputy Commander relayed messages in an improvised manner. The feathered "smoking" engine was restarted and provided partial power at a lower altitude, and we arrived at the home base without further incident, although landing was difficult in a crosswind.

Examination indicated that our electrical system and communication system had been badly damaged, causing radio transmission to be garbled. The "smoking" in engine #3 was apparently caused by burning oil fluids from the damaged #4 engine. If anything malfunctioned, it always seemed to be in those tight moments on a bomb run over the target.

Information from headquarters reached us that Orders had been amended, cutting
the tour of duty for Lead Command Aircrews to 30 missions. We had passed the halfway
mark.

Mission 17 Complete

Flak Valley

Along the Rhine River in Western Germany is the Ruhr Valley. Germany had established an expansive industrial system in this Valley. Within this industrial system were elaborate anti-aircraft installations. The anti-aircraft flak fire was so heavy, the Air Force called the Ruhr Valley, *Flak Valley*. We were called upon only occasionally when pinpoint bombing (ability to place bombs on a specific spot) was required.

On the 26th of August 1944, our briefed target was in Flak Valley, a place called Gelsenkirchen, Germany. Our primary target was a small oil refinery that apparently was supplying fuel and lubricants to the German troops in the west.

Since heavy anti-aircraft defenses were anticipated, our bombing altitude was raised to 29,000 feet. Our route was designed to feint at Bremen, then turn south for the true attack on Gelsenkirchen. The target was covered with a smoke screen, which combined with poor visibility, made it difficult to find. The sighting troubles, as well as the planned short bomb run to limit damage from anti-aircraft fire, caused us to change our target. We destroyed another industrial installation of significant importance instead.

Flak was heavy. A remark from the Navigator passed through the intercom as we left the target area, "Those Krauts threw everything at us but the kitchen sink." The Bombardier countered immediately with, "Well, Wally, I didn't see the kitchen sink, but the faucets for one passed us about a minute ago." We encountered 155-mm heavy anti-aircraft fire for the first time. We were more familiar with 88mm and 105-mm anti-aircraft fire. Ten percent (6 B-17G's) of our 91st Group aircraft were lost to anti-aircraft on this mission, with only a few parachutes witnessed, and a large number of crewmembers were listed as casualties.

I had two close encounters with pieces of flak that day—one about 6 inches under my left leg, the other was caught in my flak vest. My crew was uninjured however, and we returned from Flak Valley with a healthy respect for defenses in the Ruhr.

Friend or Foe

As the War progressed in 1944 and more and more B-17's were lost in Germany, a puzzling problem occurred. Not all B-17's were completely destroyed. Some B-17's obviously crash-landed, but were not totally demolished. The Germans could salvage parts from these planes and eventually the Germans could reconstruct a flyable B-17 manned by a German aircrew.

It was conceivable that a B-17, crewed by Germans, could feign a flight problem and attempt to join a returning 8th Air Force Group formation. Once in the formation, the German-crewed B-17 could blast the returning formation with devastating results.

Lead Command Pilots try desperately to maneuver formations to assist damaged B-17's that obviously were struggling. Damaged B-17's usually had difficulty holding formation at altitude if one or more engines were damaged. Without protection of the Group formation firepower, B-17's were easy prey to marauding enemy fighters.

It was reported in mid-August that a Group formation lost over a dozen planes to a *rogue* German B-17. The rogue German B-17 *feathered* an inboard engine to look damaged and was allowed to join the Group formation. It proceeded to the Command center position in the formation where it opened fire on the Lead Command B-17 and others. It then restarted its engine and dove out of the formation. The rogue B-17 was destroyed, but not until the German crew parachuted out. Rogue German B-17's presented a realistic stratagem that seriously worried Lead Commanders.

Radio confirmation of *enemy or foe* was also a problem, since radio equipment was often damaged and could neither receive nor broadcast. It was finally concluded that B-17's without positive confirmation could not be allowed to join established formations. Lead Group Commanders were authorized to shoot down rejoining B-17's in defense of their formations. This presented some heart-wrenching decisions.

I had probably a dozen damaged B-17's join my formations, but in all cases, positive identification was made. I usually called for our *Little Friends* to provide escort for questionable B-17's trying to join an established formation. Also, all aircraft in my formations were directed to target the joining B-17. It was a worry, but defense of the formation was a primary responsibility.

"A Tough One"

A bomb crew in every "tour" had an early mission where it experienced more difficulty than any other in the past. "Our day" was on the 8th of September 1944,—the target, a synthetic factory at Ludwigshaven, Germany—Mission 19.

Briefing was routine, our route was excellent, and we encountered no German fighter aircraft. The weather, however, was a negative influencing factor. As winter was setting in, we were beginning to experience difficulty in "fixing" our bombsights on the target due to clouds covering our "aiming point". USSTAF (Bombing Command) had ordered blind-bombing units (Mickey Sets) installed into the *Lead Command* B-17G's for use when target "aiming points" could not be identified visually.

On this day, a scouting Mosquito reported that the target was obscured, so Mission Orders were to make a bomb run with our "Mickey" blind-bombing device. We encountered no flak as we turned on the IP and entered the bomb run. Suddenly, we saw our target visually as the clouds opened for us. The sky blackened with flak bursts and the sky literally exploded—partially from the flak and partially from our own *B-17G's*.

We were "hard hit"—our "Lead"B-17G' with heavy battle damage, our waist gunner, S/Sgt. Milton Pitts had his right shoulder injured, the Mickey Operator,1st Lt. Gordon Lowe, had his leg pierced by four pieces of flak, and our tail gunner was hit in the head, but not seriously. In spite of his serious injury, Lt. Lowe continued to identify the target "aiming point" and to release the bomb load accurately on target. He was later promoted to Captain and received a Distinguished Flying Cross (DFC).

As flak centered about the Lead Command B-17G as we turned away from the target area, my two wingmen left the formation with engines smoking. In a following formation, Lt. Weeks had been injured and had lost the use of his left hand—his co-pilot had been killed. Lt. McCarty exploded. Lt. O'Toole had been severely injured——his foot almost amputated by flak. Lt. Beasley had been severely hit in the head—his skull cracked with a burst from above—his co-pilot, killed (his engineer flew the B-17G back to the Base). Others were lost or injured, but those mentioned were among my immediate friends.

Twenty percent (20%) of the attacking aircraft were lost near the target area—an additional ten (10%) crashed or didn't return to Base. Of the remaining aircraft, only several had no wounded aboard.

The medics had a busy day when we returned—ambulances had to make two trips to handle all the wounded. Most of the B-17G's were only skeletons—framework with engines attached. Many of the B-17G's landed with tires flat, engines with feathered propellers, longerons and wing spars cracked, and extreme aircraft skin damage.

Although we destroyed our target, we paid a high price for "one synthetic factory".

I shall never forget the 8th of September 1944, for I was as close to death as I had ever been in air combat to date. Following this mission, we were "down" (didn't fly) for two weeks as our aircraft were being repaired or replaced. We trained new replacement crews to replace lost aircrews, visited the Base Hospital nearby, and *"licked our wounds"*. *Mission 19 "behind us"!*

A Birthday Party

The 91st Bomb Group was one of the very first of our American (H) Heavy Bombardment units to operate in England in the European Theater of Operation (ETO). On September 15th, 1944, we celebrated our second year of combat operation. Extensive preparations were made for the festive occasion, and the countryside was invited to participate. Two hundred English young ladies from London were invited to our dance. An Orchestra for the Officers and one big name band for the Enlisted Men were imported from London. A carnival with all the paraphernalia was set up on the Field outside the Enlisted Men's barracks. It was a celebration of celebrations—a festival of festivals.

Lager and stronger spirits flowed freely. We forgot air combat for two days—a day and the morning after. Suddenly it was over, and we prepared to go back to the task of bombing. The debris was collected, the Field returned to normalcy, or as near as could be expected, and Bassingbourn's 91st Bomb Group returned to War.

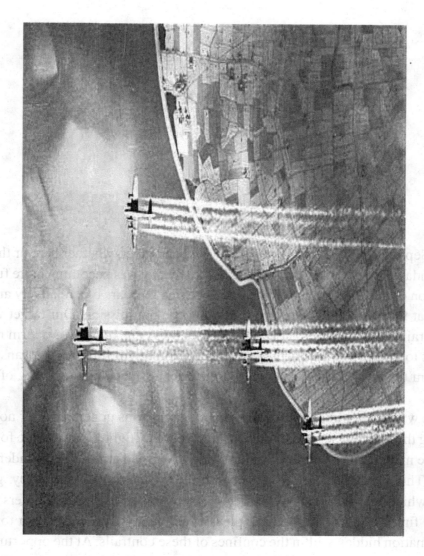

"FLYING FORMATION"

Choke Point

The 19th of September 1944 is a day I will always remember, whether here or there, for this was my birthday. Two events in my life, which day-by-day was becoming more full, prefaced the conclusion of this day. It marked the day I became 26 years old, relatively an old age for active combat flyers, and it also marked my 20th combat mission. Our target was a *choke point* in the railway-yard system at Hamm, Germany. A *choke point* is a term meaning the entry or exit to a railway yard. A properly placed bomb will immobilize transportation of materiel from the area, thereby leaving the materiel at the complete mercy of subsequent attacks.

Winter was setting in quickly in Europe. Weather was generally poor now. We were experiencing the phenomena of contrails on almost every flight. Contrails are fog-like vapor trails that are manufactured by the aircraft flying in rarified atmospheres under specific air conditions. Though these contrails are beautiful to witness, they are wispy, ghost-tracks in the sky, which restrict visibility, indicate our positions to enemy fighters, and attract anti-aircraft fire. Furthermore, nothing pleased an enemy flyer more than to approach a bomber formation hidden within the confines of these contrails. At the opportune moment, the fighter attacks the unsuspecting bomber with machine-gun and cannon fire. Contrails were a problem that made winter combat flying difficult for many reasons.

We approached the target from the south at 25,000 feet, but the target was obscured by the persistent contrails of preceding bombing formations. Our decision prompted us to lose 2000 feet, "turn back", and approach the target for a second bomb run—this is called *"making a 360"*. In the process of bombing, the formation manipulates a 360-degree turn, a circle, to obtain finer bombing results.

Flak was light on our first approach to the target. The intensity as expected, was greater on the second try, so we incurred more critical battle damage. Several B-17G's were lost, while several others incurred damage leading to "crash" and "belly" landings in England. The bombing results were excellent.

The return route was made all the more difficult by contrails until we were able to drop from higher altitude where contrails disappeared. Now I was nearing the end of my air combat.

Mission 20 Complete.

Bomb by Mickey-Set

The Rhine river in the southern Ruhr Valley of Western Germany was one of the main arterial approaches to Germany's armies in the west. Through Cologne, Germany passed gasoline and oil to fuel the enemy's war machines. Ammunition and parts and materiel to oppose a pursuing Allied Force flowed relentlessly. Cologne was bombed many times and the arterial approaches were usually the target.

On the 27th of September 1944 the target was the main railway yard in Cologne. Weather was poor and the mission depended on radar blind-bombing equipment, known as the *Mickey-Set*. Our bombing altitude was 25,000 feet. The entire Bomb Group formation – now reduced to 36 aircraft – was to release bombs as the Command *Lead* B-17G (with the Mickey-Set) released its bombs.

Now that we had gained experience, the mission was strictly routine in nature – route, IP, the bomb run, bombs away, rally, return route, let-down, and home. The target was bombed with results unobserved. Practically the only way we knew that we were even in the neighborhood of the target was the opposing enemy anti-aircraft fire.

Flak was heavy but the damage was minor due to the use of chaff that disrupted the enemy radar gun sighting. Two aircraft, however, were damaged by several bursts that found the formation seemingly by chance. Both of these aircraft crash-landed in France within friendly territory.

This was our 21st mission but it was also our first in a new

aircraft that had been assigned to me—my third *B-17G*. This mission impressed me because it was carried out in a very efficient manner. It seemed like all was right. Each man performed his task with excellence. This was our first trip to Cologne, Germany, and we considered it a rather easy target.

Our next mission was to the same target about two weeks later after the Germans had just completed repairs. They had devised new defenses, and our opinion changed with respect to the vulnerability of Cologne and its opposition to heavy bomber attack.

Mouser and Dimple-S-Sally

Weather had set in now, and drizzle, low clouds, and already low temperatures were prompting us to change our summer combat flying equipment for the warmer, more protective winter equipment. We also had more time to think.

Sometimes I felt that thinking was one of the hardest of all the many elements of a combat mission—the conception of what might happen, of what had happened, wondering. We had more time to sit around while nature flexed its might with winds, fog, rain, and the likes that England is famous for. Poker games started, and the stakes were high. Bets were paid off— experience had taught us already that IOU's, amounting to thousands of dollars, had been lost over Germany.

Our fancies found new directions. For example, we had accumulated two new pets in our Command Pilot House, a cat and a dog. The dog was a female police dog that we called *Dimple-S-Sally* – only a puppy and more a task sometimes than a pleasure. When Dimple-S-Sally was a pleasure, she belonged to her appointed daddy, Uncle Robert – the good Captain Crans.

The cat was one we pilfered from the mess hall when we began noticing our trifles and rations disappearing to the mice and rats. Whether it was a she-cat or a he-cat was a topic of conversation and controversy. I truthfully can't remember ever coming to a decision.

Nevertheless, our new feline constituent was called *Mouser*, in view of its newly appointed responsibilities.

Mouser was a monstrous cat, a miniature lion. Regardless of its previous surroundings, it deserted the mess hall for the fare in our Command Pilot House. Mouser was a good cat, but we often suspected its prodigal tendencies. It would often disappear for several days at a time, only to return until the next time its tendencies became an over-riding influence.

Sometimes the weather would temporarily break for several hours. On these days we practiced formation and gunnery. There were times that I thought these gunnery exercises over the North Sea were more hazardous than combat missions. We seldom returned without battle damage to a few aircraft, as the gunners, usually new replacement gunners, became over-anxious. A gunner on one practice flight mission perforated my tail section with a few neat 50-caliber machine-gun holes, and still on another, I had my right aileron practically blown off due to a miscalculation of a turret gunner. On an unscheduled practice formation flight we sneaked up into Scotland for a sightseeing tour, and we saw the beautiful countryside. We had an accounting when we returned, but we still enjoyed the flight.

It was during this period while on a practice night flight, that another friend, Lt. DeLisle, was killed with his aircrew. The circumstances of the crash were unexplainable. Several of us grieved about the incident, but sadly "life and death" had become a routine matter now.

New responsibilities within the Squadron were assigned. Our Squadron had acquired a new Commanding Officer, Captain Immanuel J. Klette. Though he was often strict, he was fair and competent. My responsibilities had enlarged to Assistant Operations Officer, Squadron Flight Acceptance Pilot, in addition to "A" Flight Lead Command Pilot. I very seldom flew a mission now with less than 36 aircraft behind me. I had already led the 8th Air Force as Lead Command Pilot with 1,200 aircraft behind me.

As yet not one of the aircrews in our Squadron had completed a tour of duty. Orders were soon forthcoming to send home partial crews, although their tours were incomplete – psychological cases. We had now a well-balanced Squadron with a reasonable amount of experience in contrast to the early days in June, 1944. Of all the replacement crews entering the Squadron in June through August 1944, only five were left. We were in our *twenties* of accredited missions. Things were running smoothly. We were proud of our well-knit organization.

Though we spent many evenings reminiscing, we also spent many sleepless nights during this period, for time rested heavily on us. It was almost a welcome relief to "go out" again, to relieve like a safety valve the pent-up emotions that were within us. Death and destruction were impacting our psyche, and we still had a way to go.

Watch Out Below

Losses to anti-aircraft fire were high as we proceeded into middle October, 1944. Regardless of our counter-measures we were being tracked by enemy anti-aircraft firepower. The armchair experts devised a plan whereby it was presumed we could chagrin the enemy flak gunners.

The Force was estimated to amount to 1,000 aircraft, of which 500 aircraft were to comprise the "A" Force, and 500 aircraft, the "B" Force. I was scheduled to lead the "B" Force.

The plan was simply to place both Forces over the target at different altitudes. The "A" tactical Force at 25000 feet trailed slightly below the "B" tactical Force at 27000 feet. Preceding all units would be a single formation of 36 aircraft carrying a load of *chaff* with no bombs. Theoretically, the bombs from the "B" Force would fall slightly ahead of the "A" Force with a small chance of our bombs striking our own aircraft. In view of the requirements for such precise timing, I still wonder how conclusions to this effect could be made. It was controversial.

On the 15th of October 1944, our target was the rail yards at Cologne, Germany. The mission route was over France and was without incident. Timing in this plan was to be exact; otherwise, the plan was not practical. As we approached the target, the "A" Force was late, so we attempted to lose time to adjust the bomb run to a simultaneous attack. "A" Force lost more time, and no alternative was left but to attack.

The timing of the Force was now off, although the "B" Force regained its relative timing. We were over the target 10 seconds ahead of planned time of bomb release.

Flak was extremely heavy, and one section of our formation was hit hard - two were "down" over Germany and three crashed in France. Figuratively speaking, we all limped home.

We returned to our Base without further incident. We had hit our target, but the plan had not worked. A General met us in interrogation and demanded an answer as to why the plan had not been carried out as planned. Apparently he was ill-advised, for we were with him for less than five minutes. We were pleased when he departed. The plan was discarded—the extremely minute detail of the plan and the precise timing were impractical. In our experienced viewpoint, we agreed and made it known!

This was the end of a strange mission, but the results had been obtained. The mission was successful, although the strategy was not.

Psychological Problems

It was seldom discussed, but as air combat experience increased, the phantom of psychological trauma became a potential problem. Often it was unnoticed because the person hid the tell-tale anguished symptoms for fear that among his peers it would be interpreted as a sign of personal weakness. Documentation of a psychological problem in his personnel file would be a real career-breaker.

Suicides became more than a passing event as the air combat conditions in mid-1944 became fierce and more demanding during the deep-penetration missions.

Although there were a number of cases, I will recall only one personal experience with a young replacement pilot who I will not name. I was disappointed in his loose formation flying and visited his room *to "kick butt"* and sentence him to several practice formation sessions. When I knocked and entered his room, he was standing on his bed with his 45-caliber pistol in his ear. I startled him (which could have been disastrous) but he lowered his pistol, and asked, "What do YOU want?" It was a tense and unexpected moment, so I changed my subject, telling him I had some *terrific good news that wouldn't wait*! He respected me, and we had a long talk. He received medical attention and was sent home shortly thereafter.

There were cases of alcoholism, abusive behavior, discipline misbehavior, and actual physical sickness beyond nausea. It probably will always be a problem in War, even for very fit human beings.

Catastrophe

While bomber combat crews sweated through their missions, it was odd how incidences were cyclic. For several weeks the losses were relatively low, then, a period of heavy losses ensued. Seemingly the new crews were lost, then the veteran crews. It was as the unfolding of a prescribed plan for loss and gain. There were periods when the cycles ran for several weeks, even a month at times. Between the 1st of October and mid-November, 1944, we entered one of these periods of heavy losses—mostly involving inexperienced new replacement crews. The assigned targets during this period of the War were usually heavily protected by anti-aircraft defenses. Also, the enemy fighters were suddenly opposing our deep-penetration efforts with more regularity than usual.

Catastrophe struck at the 91st Bomb Group twice within a week—the total losses for this period were close to 25 complete aircrews. Several small barracks were vacated as one Squadron suffered the wrath of the enemy. It was as if an ill wind had stealthily whisked the occupants away with scarcely as much as a whisper. Half-completed letters, unfinished handiwork, and books opened face down where reading had stopped lay undisturbed. There was something supernatural and ominous about a whole barracks being emptied.

I particularly remember a young pilot, Lt. Milligan, scarcely 20 years old, who had a *feeling* that this was his last. The night preceding the mission he came to several of us with, "If anything should happen—you know——you, "Collie" take my trench coat; you, "Brownie" take my radio; and you "Bobby", can have my model airplane". Lt. Milligan exploded over the target scarcely twelve hours later - another of those odd circumstances of fate.

Premonitions of airmen happened time-and-time again. In the beginning we shrugged the feelings away, but in time we were silent and wondered.

"Wing Hit"

Nightmares

There is a macabre fascination in War and air-combat that is more a feeling than a description. As a person enters combat for the first time after months and years of preparatory practice, the first shots or bursts of flak that whistle through the cockpit signals a solemn realization that the enemy means to "kill ya". Air combat is a treacherous game of "life and death" that plays out with an awesome consequence to young men and women, their families and the country. World War II is an ultimate case history of the deadly game of air combat played a half century ago.

The B-17 (H) Heavy Bomber deep penetrations into Germany (1943-1945) are grim examples of "risk and consequence". The opposition of a war-competent enemy, operating technically advanced equipment while implementing a well thought-out strategy, dramatically increases the stakes in the conflict and difficulty of survival.

Remember, failure in this game is death!

There are a myriad of feelings that dominate the psyche as experience develops in this deadly game of air-combat.

<u>Fear</u> enters the mind when death is close or imminent.

<u>Horror</u> wells in one's mind as one witnesses the mutilation of human bodies, some friends you laughed and shared thoughts with the prior night.

<u>Sadness</u> occurs in the aftermath of a mission, as an accounting of loss and damage spells out the consequence.

All of the emotions resulting from the indelible horrifying memories interact with contemplations of the next mission. The nightmares that cloud one's sleep are revelations of the inner conflicts of air-combat in one's mind.

As an example, come with me on a final trip!

The B-17G (H) Heavy Bomber is flying easily in a Vee formation at 25,000 feet as the Group formation approaches a munitions factory target 80 miles southwest of Berlin, Germany. Out of the quiet, anti-aircraft flak bursts suddenly occur, and the formation executes small maneuvers as evasive action. As if from out of nowhere, there is a blinding burst and flash which jolts the B-17G. The plane vibrates uncontrollably as the very sounds of pieces of flak whistle and penetrates the skin and interior of the B-17. Suddenly, a large outboard section of the wing twists away as the fractured wing-spars separate.

All this, happening in seconds.

The B-17G veers slowly at first "away" from the missing wing section from aerodynamic drag and noses down. The pilot desperately manipulates the flight controls to bring the B-17G upright and level. As his effort fails and the B-17 starts a slow spin downward the pilot pounds the rudder and yoke with ultimate frustration...

The B-17 is clearly out of control!

Through the intercom, the pilot issues orders to "bail out!" The B-17G has now increased in speed of descent to alarming proportions and the spinning action continues.

The aircrew, all ten, realizing the catastrophic situation, attempt to scramble to their respective escape hatches and attempt to evacuate the turrets. When they release their safety belts and harnesses, however, they start tumbling for lack of handholds and the force. The spinning centrifugal force accentuates the difficulties as it forces their bodies against the structure. The men's body weight increases (500-800 pounds/ man) due to "g" forces, as the B-17G now is plummeting earthward. The "g" force (effect of acceleration and gravity) come into play even further.

Muscles are unable to move the body easily.

The escape hatches are in sight, but impossible to reach.

Equipment is breaking loose.

Debris is flying lethally in all directions.

Stop and think...after almost 5 miles of spinning free-fall and "what may seem forever" in a trapped area, unable to reach the escape hatches, panic is overwhelming! The myriad of fears increase with the fruitless struggle to escape, and frustration overwhelms all senses! The understanding of the finality of this event has now become obvious... No Escape.

ETERNITY.

Unsung Heroes

One of the most important, but under-praised efforts in the air wars of the European Theater of Operation (ETO) were the magnificent and dedicated ground crews who kept the war aircraft flying.

The nights and days before a mission were hectic with a myriad of skin and structural repairs, engine replacements, fueling, armament installation, bomb loading, instrument repair and check-out, etc. Success of a mission depended not only on pilot and aircrew skills, but reliable operation of the aircraft and its equipment. The refurbishment of an aircraft returning from a mission was often accomplished in rain and chilling cold, since hangars were limited for repair of the host of damaged aircraft in an 8th Air Force Air Group. It seemed always a fight against time to ready a damaged aircraft for the next mission. It was a magnificent effort well done.

Pilots were grateful for a well-trained ground crew. During training flights between missions, pilots scheduled pleasure flights for their ground crews when practical. It was a popular event.

Buzzing

The Air Force defined *"buzzing"* as the manipulation of aircraft within the close proximity of the ground with no intention of enacting a landing. This maneuver was prohibited, but circumstances often left no alternative. A broad outlook on buzzing was observed in the combat areas. On the 25th of October 1944, we had cause to "buzz" the English countryside with justification.

The target was the dock installations on the outskirts of the city of Hamburg, Germany. Weather obscured our target, so our bombs were aimed by our blind-bombing device, our *Mickey-Set*. The result of our bombing was excellent. The point bombs fell scarcely more than 100 yards from the expected mean point of impact. Our losses were light, and the flak damage negligible. Frontal weather activity caused concern on the return route. Before approaching the coastline of England, we were *"on the deck"*—flying at very low altitude. As we passed over the coastline and vectored our formation to our Base, we were scarcely more than treetop level and still in formation.

I can only imagine the sight as 36 four-engine *Flying Fortresses* grazed the rooftops in formation, and the deafening roar as the planes materialized from the mist and haze as ghost ships and disappeared practically as they had come.

Finding

Finding the landing strip was always a difficult task in restricted visibility, and it was amazing how collisions were avoided as the aircraft milled about the field. A 20-30 ton mass of metal hurtling through the sky at 3-4 miles a minute isn't as flexible to maneuver as first observation might reflect.

Skin and Throttles

Our target on the 5th of November 1944 was a specific factory area in Frankfort, Germany. Flak was moderate, and we lost no aircraft. Flak damage, however, was considerable. Our target was partially destroyed, with results termed fair. Both routes *in and out* were excellent and the bombs were released visually. For once the weather was not a handicap to our bombing. The impression I retain of this mission was the sub-zero, bitter, bone-aching cold, for the heating unit became inoperative soon after take-off.

Leading the formation, I usually employed the automatic pilot called *"George"* by most combat pilots. To gain the most effectiveness from "George", over 22 switches and knobs had to be minutely adjusted as conditions of load, weight-balance, aircraft attitude, air roughness and altitude varied. As we neared the target, I found that my heavy winter flying gloves impeded these adjustments, so I removed my right-hand glove to manipulate the small switches and knobs. The temperature was close to 55 degrees(F) below zero. An autopilot oscillating condition at the moment diverted attention from the temperature, and I felt no immediate discomfort—I should have known better and been warned by this alone. A throttle adjustment was necessary, so I quickly reached up to grasp the four throttles in the quadrant. As I grasped the quadrant and subsequently released, or rather tried to release the throttles, I found my right hand had partially frozen on the controls. I wrenched my hand away, but left flesh and skin clinging to the cold metal.

I had no feeling in my hand, so there was no immediate pain. My co-pilot assumed temporary control of the aircraft at my direction. I placed my frozen right hand under my left arm next to the body, gradually warming the palm of my hand with body heat. Feeling tingled and seeped achingly back to my hand. I was uncomfortable and chagrined at my own thoughtless undoing. Fortunately the damage was superficial—except for discomfort, I suffered no permanent injury.

Cold was one of our bitter winter enemies. Particular emphasis was placed on precautionary measures to avoid freezing and frostbite. In bad cases of frostbite, surgical amputation of areas afflicted was common. I gained a healthy respect through this experience for the hypocritical nature of extreme cold.

Mission 24 was complete.

Swordfish-Able-Leader

"Survival" in bomber air operations directly relates to minimum time in the defended enemy target area. Within limits of formation control, evasive action to avoid excessive anti-aircraft flak damage is critical. During all these flying actions, altitude and speed of the formation requires close control with focus on the target, IP, and bomb-release point.

Following bomb-release, escape maneuvers guide the formation out of the explosive target area. Invariably, after bomb-release, the Group formations spread out due to battle damage and evasive action. The *Lead Command* Pilot analyzes the situation quickly and executes appropriate maneuvers to close the formation. It is imperative to accomplish re-formation quickly, since enemy fighter aircraft generally position themselves just outside the anti-aircraft flak area to pick-off damaged bombers not flying in formation.

Experience taught us that enemy fighter aircraft invariably preferred to attack loose or spread formations, since the bomber formation firepower diminishes rapidly as the formation spreads. Lead Command Pilot requirements are extremely difficult on heavily defended targets. Once committed to attack, the aircrews *"bet their lives"* on the flying skills, experience and presence-of-mind of the Lead Command Pilot. Even with experienced Lead Command Pilots, losses can be devastating due to target variables and the level of enemy opposition. Each Lead Pilot Commander had a pseudonym.

Mine was SWORDFISH–ABLE-LEADER.

Citations

The Military Services recognize outstanding valor in combat by (1) Commendations by Commanding Officers and (2) Medals. The most awarded USAF air combat medals in the ETO were: The Distinguished Flying Cross (DFC), The Air Medal (AM), and, for those wounded, The Purple Heart (PH). The most coveted reward for valor "beyond-the-expected" was the "Medal of Honor", which was rarely awarded (less than 17) in the 8th Air Force (ETO) for unknown reasons.

It was an enigma to many of us that there was so little use of the "Medal of Honor" to recognize valor, when an estimated 26,000 or more airmen were killed in these missions. There were clearly more heroic incidents and bravery than were recognized by award of this high level medal in the USAF (ETO). The large number of (H) Heavy Bombers in the 8th Air Force and the large aircrew population risking daily "casualty and death" in air combat and the bombing of highly-defended targets emphasizes this point—"surely someone was heroic"!

Veterans of the WWII era have been conspicuous in their silence. For the most part, civilians, under direction of professionals, executed the military stratagems in WWII. The civilian soldiers seldom expressed thoughts of a future military career. Most civilian soldiers were focused on "just getting the present job done"!

The medal award program in combat areas was informal and inconspicuous. The usual occurrence was notification of an award and subsequent release of a brief news item for the veteran's local newspaper. The medal awards eventually appeared in the veteran's permanent personnel file. In the gross administration of data in a combat operation, permanent personnel files may not have been totally accurate or complete. Notifications of awards were sometimes made, but upon Separation of Service, the awards were not totally included. There were probably many reasons for this. Foremost, the conduct of war operations had priority. The "paperwork" was voluminous and secondary in many Commands, which invited errors and omissions as the intensity of the war increased.

The medal program did not particularly impress most active air combat veterans. The awards of Distinguished Flying Crosses and Air Medals and Purple Hearts seemed to be almost automatic—everybody had these medals. On the other hand, practically no one heard of higher medal awards, deserved or not.

There were literally no complaints, since in the view of most aircrew veterans "survival" was the real reward! In fact, "heroics" were commonplace and "citations for bravery" often seemed, at the time, to be an overstatement and embarrassing!

I was officially awarded (3) three Distinguished Flying Crosses (DFC'S), (5) five Air Medals (AM's) and a Commendation by General Doolittle, USAF Commander, 8th Air Force,:——-"For your outstanding efforts and personal bravery in carrying out the tasks assigned under grave and insurmountable difficulties."

The Commendation related to the "unplanned" and "in-flight" decision by the 91st Bomb Group Lead Command Pilot "Team" to attack a highly-defended Merseburg Oil and Refinery Complex at"low level" (17,000 feet) in November, 1944, to assure its destruction.

The 91st Bomb Group was assigned "Lead" of an Air Force of over 1,000 B-17G's, with orders to destroy the Merseburg Oil and Refinery Complex with a bombing attack at 29,000 feet. The high altitude of 29,000 feet was selected to avoid high B-17G losses and crippling battle damage while attacking this highly-defended target. Past missions had been unsuccessful in totally damaging the refinery. Anti-air defense and Luftwaffe attacks had been devastating, and fuel continued to flow to the German Armies. Destruction of the Merseburg Oil and Refinery Complex was critically important to the Allied Ground Forces, since it was primary in supplying fuel and oil to motorized German units and tanks in southwest Europe, particularly the "Bulge, where heavy Allied casualties and other extreme difficulties were being experienced in advancing into Germany.

It is estimated that less than three Bomb Groups (approximately 100 B-17'Gs) of the estimated 1000 B-17G Bombers attacked Merseburg Oil and Refinery Complex. Other 8th Air Force Bomb Groups on this mission selected other "targets of opportunity" when the planned conditions of attack at 27,000 feet and foul weather suggested that mission success was improbable—this "decision" was their "right" in air combat protocol. The probability of accurate bombing to destroy this difficult Merseburg Oil and Refinery Complex target at 27,000 foot altitude without "visual targeting" was very poor. The cloud level was 17,500 feet, so "visual targeting" meant a bomb attack at an altitude lower than 17,500 feet—this was "suicide" on a highly defended target, such as Merseburg..

When the three Groups selected to attack Merseburg visually at the 17,000 foot level, it was known that the aircrew losses and B-17G losses and battle damage would be immense. In spite of the "suicide" nature of the bomb assault, the 8th Air Force Lead Group, the 91st Bomb Group, and two others(approximately 100 B-17G Bombers) made this attack. The surprise of the low-level bombing assault and the resultant bombing accuracy at 17,000 feet destroyed the Merseburg Oil and Refinery Complex "once and for all"!

Less than 65 B-17G Bombers, of the 100 B-17G Bombers, survived the bomb attack at this low level, but this high-priority target, Merseburg Oil and Refinery Complex, had been finally destroyed and probably saved hundreds of allied ground troop lives.

In later analysis, it probably shortened World War II in the ETO. Within 30 days, German motorized equipment, including tanks, were being left in the fighting area—"out-of fuel"!

The Commendation and notation of this mission, somehow, never found the "permanent personnel files" of any of the survivors, or participants in this important, "voluntary", and "dreadfully dangerous" mission. Since the low-level bombing attack was an "in flight" and "improvised" mission attack (from the planned mission attack at 27,000 feet), it is not clear that it was even recorded in 8th Air Force documentation.

The vagaries of Medal Awards and Commendations are that acts of heroism, or bravery, or conspicuous gallantry often aren't reported, or the incidents are lost in *getting on* with the War".

Nevertheless, while citations and medals and commendations were part of our personal war history, they were a "side issue", not a personnel objective.

Mission Briefing

It was the middle of the night and small groups of young aircrews file toward a roughly-constructed building appropriately called the mission-briefing hut. The pilots and co-pilots enter the building and stand in small groups scanning the walls and covered map at the end of the room. The interior of the mission briefing hut has seats for 100-150 people, the huge map at the end of the room covers England, France and Germany and obviously pictures the mission route, but it is now covered. A briefing podium stands in front of the covered map. The right wall displays the entire Group formations with each B-17G shown by an aircraft symbol. Each B-17G symbol has a First Pilot's name, his aircraft alphanumeric identification and his relative position in the formation. The left wall presents in bold letters the parameters of the mission – engine start time, taxi-time, take-off intervals, assembly altitude, codes, etc. Each pilot carries a small flight log to record significant mission information that relates to his flight.

The briefing starts at a precise time with "Attention" called out by the Master Sergeant responsible for the briefing room. All the aircrew members rise as the Group Briefing Officers enter. Major Reid enters the room and approaches the briefing podium. He faces the aircrews and says, "Gentlemen, be seated."

The screen covering the huge map behind Major Reid slowly rises and deep red lines indicate the mission route and bold alphabetic letters indicate the checkpoints en-route to the target.

Major Reid continues, "The target today is Merseburg – the oil and fuel refinery complex". The aircrews groan as they recognize the target as one of the most highly defended targets in Germany.

Major Reid then addresses the huge map and traces the mission route with a long pointer. He explains each major point in the route with a final warning, "Note Checkpoint Charlie. There is a narrow corridor between major German anti-aircraft installations that are critically dangerous. Transit Checkpoint Charlie at 27,000 feet, since this is your planned Initial Point (IP) and bombing altitude. The bomb run is only minutes away. The refinery target is long and narrow, so navigate the bomb run direction as planned to optimize bomb deployment.

Major Reid then addresses the left wall of the briefing hut and continues, "Mission parameters are posted as follows," as he points out engine start times and the priorities for take-off, etc. He then announces, "Take-off will be on runway Able on a heading of 248 degrees and assembly will be over the Bassingbourn Marker at 15,000 feet. Your assembly recognition flare will be "RED-RED". He then addresses the right wall and notes details of the formation; "The 324th Bomb Squadron is the designated Lead-Command formation. The 401st will fly high formation. The 323rd will fly low formation. Code name for your Lead Command will be *Swordfish Able Leader*. '*Recall*', if necessary, will be received in code, '*Hot Time Tonight.*' Your Radio Operators will have specific instructions for '*Strike Time*,' and will report status and first assessment of strike damage."

Major Reid continued, "Intelligence informs us that intense enemy opposition can be expected before, during, and after your bomb-run. Luftwaffe fighter squadrons ate stationed nearby, so prepare for fighter attack before and after the bomb-run. Merseburg is the most important remaining fuel and oil supply for German motorized units, and the Germans are fully aware of the importance of this critical facility for continuance of the war."

He continued, "Meteorology reports a rapidly advancing cold front that will challenge your mission today. Listen for 'Angels' or 'Devils' to denote altitude change of assembly altitude if the formation assembly incurs weather or visibility problems. Reconnaissance reports broken clouds in the target area, but the weather changes rapidly this time of year. Winds at target altitude are estimated at 80 knots at 210 degrees (from the west). Temperature is estimated at minus 52 degrees F."

Major Reid then noted, "The leading formations will carry 1000 pound and 500 pound general purpose (GP) bombs, while the following formations will carry incendiary bombs. Check with your armament crew chief for armament details. Your bomb loads are selected to penetrate and shatter the refinery installations, while the incendiaries will start heavy fires. Merseburg is vulnerable to fire."

Major Reid then proceeds beck to the podium and asks, "Any questions, Gentlemen?"After a brief interchange, Major Reid stands aside.

At this time, the 91st Bomb Group Commander, Colonel Terry takes the stage. "Gentlemen, this is a vitally important target. Destruction of this target is critically important to the success of the invasion of our Allied Forces. The Germans with their motorized units and short supply lines are 'kicking butt' on our ground forces in the Bulge. Men, you can do something about it! Make no mistake; the Germans know the importance of Merseburg. Expect heavy opposition. I expect your best efforts. Good luck!"

As Colonel Terry leaves the podium, the Chaplain advances to the front of the room and prays for safe delivery of the aircrews.

Major Reid takes the stage again and says, "Synchronize your watches. It is now 0240 hours, any further questions?If not, good luck!"

The mission briefing is complete. The airmen make final notes in their logs, rise and file in small groups to their respective equipment huts to dress for the mission.

The mission has begun.

Merseberg Oil and Refinery Complex— Suicide

Perhaps the most hated and feared enemy target in all of Germany in late 1944 was the Merseburg Oil and Refinery Complex. As the war progressed, as the enemy became more desperate for fuel and oil to service its motorized units, defenses of its vital refinery resources increased proportionately. The Merseburg Oil and Refinery Complex was perhaps the most heavily defended target in all of Germany at this particular time.

In late 1944, USAF Strategic Command generally felt that aircraft and aircrew losses incurred by an open visual (H) Heavy Bomber attack could not be tolerated. Several earlier 1944 high-altitude bomb missions suffered high loss and damage, yet the Merseburg Oil and Refinery Complex was not conclusively put out of commission. (H) Heavy Bomber attack was deferred, even as defenses of Merseburg continued to increase.

The effectiveness and threat of German motorized units opposing the Allied invasion of Europe in the late Fall of 1944 caused high concern and a reevaluation was made of a (H) Heavy Bomber attack on Merseburg. It was concluded that the Merseburg Oil and Refinery Complex had to be destroyed, but the "risk factor" was enormous, with probable high loss of bombers and aircrews-—perhaps as many as 2-3 Air Groups, or more. A high-altitude attack density had to be substantial for total target destruction, since the target was almost a mile-long and narrow, bending with the river alongside. Obviously, the enemy was also aware of Merseburg and intended to protect it accordingly. Nonetheless, the decision was finally made that the Merseburg Oil and Refinery Complex had to be totally destroyed.

In November, 1944, The 8th Air Force assigned the Merseburg bomb mission Lead to the 91st Bomb Group. The *Lead* Command was assigned to the 324th Bomb Squadron with Capt. Ray M. Brown, as Lead Command Pilot. Major "Manny" Klette was assigned Co-pilot and Mission Command Coordinator. Code name of the mission Lead was identified as *Swordfish-Able-Leader*.

We were briefed by USAF Strategic Command prior to this mission that **destruction** of Merseburg was **urgent** for successful progress of the Allied invasion.

The 91st Bomb Group assembled over the Bassingbourn "marker", and assumed a "pick-up" route to gather the other Bomb Groups of the mission Air Force. The assembled bomber procession headed over the English Channel and proceeded on the route described in briefing. The anti-aircraft was modest and there was no German fighter intercept until the Lead Command Group neared the target area. Even the Germans didn't like to fly in bad weather.

As the Air Force approached the Merseburg Oil and Refinery Complex and prior to the IP at 27,000 feet, cloud cover obscured the target. The consistent high level clouds and wind drift caused concern for bombing accuracy of this narrow target at this high altitude. Success of an effective bomb attack required bomb patterns from compact B-17 Group formations. Typically, only Lead aircraft carried the accurate Norden Bomb Sight and indicated the exact point for release of bombs. The remaining B-17's in each Group formation "*toggled*" the release of their bomb loads forming a destructive bomb pattern.

Attack conditions to assure high probability of a successful bomb delivery at the Merseburg target created a dilemma. The Swordfish-Able Lead Command considered these major mission options: (1) Bombing at 27,000 feet as briefed, with probable poor bombing results (2) Aborting the Merseburg mission for "*targets of opportunity*" where bombing accuracy might be less critical, or (3) *"Letting down"* the Air Force formations to lower altitudes for an accurate visual bomb run, but with probable high A/C losses and aircrew casualties. Each of the bombing Group Lead Commanders, following the 91st Bomb Group had decision options. Most of the Group formations in this Merseburg Oil and Refinery Complex mission **declined** the low-altitude attack option. Only 3 Bomb Group formations flew over the Merseburg Oil and Refinery Complex target at low altitude.

The decision to bomb successfully at other than briefed altitudes and direction requires extraordinary pilot and crew skills. Maneuvering a series of B-17G flight formations, each with 36 aircraft, after penetrating 10,000 feet of clouds, on a target for a visual bomb run is a complex flying operation. For example, when a Lead Command Pilot maneuvers large formations of aircraft through several thousand feet of lower cloud cover, it is necessary to establish steady and precise rates of decline, to execute small, but precise changes in heading, and to maintain steady speed with minimum throttle change for formation control. It also requires a practical navigation—bombing plan to exit the clouds near the beginning of a bomb run (IP) with a short time over target to minimize flak damage. These procedures must be precisely executed with anti-aircraft flak opposition and rough air.

Swordfish-Able-Leader Command made the decision to attack the Merseburg refinery complex visually at an estimated 17,000 bombing altitude. The anti-aircraft flak was intense. The visual bomb attack, however, caused devastating target damage, which was witnessed. As expected, the losses of B-17's and aircrews were large. Of the estimated 100 attacking aircraft, it was noted that probably less than 65 survived, and all surviving aircraft suffered large damage and aircrew losses.

The dialogue that follows prefaced the execution of the dangerous visual bombing attack on the Merseburg Oil and Refinery Complex:

Pilot (Brown) to Navigator (Wallace): "Are we on course and on time?"

Navigator to Pilot: "We are exactly on time and about 25 minutes to the (bombing) IP."

Pilot to Bombardier: "Can you find the target under these conditions of cloud cover?"

Bombardier to Pilot: "The target is obscured and the prevailing winds are negative for this on-line target. It is doubtful we can bomb the target accurately without a visual bomb run."

Pilot to Co-pilot/Mission Command Coordinator (Klette): "Klette, can you get the cloud base over the target with winds from weather reconnaissance quickly?"

Co-pilot to Pilot: "Roger."

Co-pilot to Pilot: "Cloud base over the target is 17,500 feet. No data on current winds. Command wants this target badly. Can we execute a visual bomb attack successfully? If we do this, we're going to get 'our ass shot off'."

Pilot to Navigator: "Wally, can you give me a navigation point to start a letdown to 17,000 feet through this cloud cover? I want to break out seconds before the IP and start the bomb-run on planned course?"

Navigator to Pilot: "Roger" Can do! "You've got to hold the formation "on course" during the letdown through these 'stinking' clouds. But, I need a decision now! We're getting close to the target area."

Pilot to Bombardier: "Ok, at 17,000 feet?"

Bombardier to Pilot: "Affirmative, but I need the PDI centered on auto-pilot before turn-in at the IP. Will you trim the 'pots' for the (bomb) run?"

Pilot to Bombardier: "Roger. It will be tight and expect heavy flak and turbulence, but consider it will be done."

Pilot to Co-pilot: "Klette, can you get a coded approval from Strategic Command for mission change to a 17,000 low level visual attack?"

Co-pilot to Pilot: "We are going to lose a lot of planes. We have to be successful."

Pilot to Co-pilot: "Affirmative. Get Command 'on the horn'."

Co-pilot to Pilot: "Mission change is approved. Let's do it!"

Pilot to Crew: "We are attacking Merseberg visually at 17,000 feet. The mission, other than altitude will be exactly as briefed."

Pilot to Navigator: "Wally, give me the precise point to start formation let-down and course. Letdown will be standard-- we've done this before!"

Navigator to Pilot: "Start let-down in exactly 3 minutes on course of 95 degrees magnetic."

Pilot to Navigator: "Roger."

Pilot to Crew: "Everybody hold tight! Here we go!"

Tail gunner to Pilot: "The formation is doing great-- everybody is in place."

Pilot to Co-pilot: "Handle the intercom--I'm going to be busy."

Co-pilot to Pilot: "Roger".

Navigator to Pilot: "We have located the target visually-- the IP is 60 seconds away. Stay on present course. Man! This was close!"

Pilot to Bombardier: "Auto-pilot pots are trimmed, bomb-bays are open, and the PDI is centered."

Bombardier to Pilot: "Roger. We're at the IP, and I have the aiming point in sight! It's mine!"

The sky literally explodes with flak. The bombers rock and roll and pitch to the hits and near misses. The sky blackens with the exploding flak. The planes in the following formations disappear in the black flak bursts and exploding debris from direct hits and exploding bombers. "Bombs Away!"Bomb-bay doors close and the flak avoidance procedure is quickly executed.

Pilot to Crew: "Report in!"

The Crew "reports in", reporting no serious injuries. The bomber is riddled by holes and missing bomber structure, but nothing catastrophic. The formation is in disarray and badly damaged. The next problem is to assemble the remaining bombers in the formation. The maneuvers and reassembly is accomplished just in time to see enemy fighters approaching ahead. The Crew calls out the approaching enemy fighters with seemingly calm precision, and the second battle is "on"! The engagement lasted for only a few minutes, and the enemy fighters turn to the damaged bombers that seemed to scatter the sky.

The anti-aircraft flak was still intense. The visual bomb attack, however, caused devastating target damage, which was witnessed. As expected the losses of B-17G's and aircrew were large. Of the estimated 100 attacking aircraft, it was estimated that only 65% survived, and those incurred large battle-damage and crewmember loss. Fighter cover arrived outside the heavy flak area as we headed for England. A battered 91st Bomb Group formation circled over the Base and the "red-red flare" B-17G's land quickly, the remainder of the bombers then land.

In debriefing of the circumstance and success of the Merseburg Oil and Refinery Complex bombing and later conversations with USAF Command, it was suggested that this was a historic mission similar to the Schweinfurt mission that the 91st Bomb Group also lead. Lt. General Doolittle, Commander of the 8th Air Force, sent a personal Commendation to Capt. Brown and Major Klette:——- "for outstanding effort and personal bravery in carrying out the task assigned under grave and seemingly insurmountable difficulties." Head quarters of the Allied Army Commands in France were exuberant in the mission success.

Three of my best friends were lost on this mission—it was a sobering thought for missions yet to be flown.

Mission 25 complete.

An Invitation

Returning from a short training flight, I found Major Klette, the 324th Bomb Squadron Commanding Officer, waiting for me. We were friends and enjoyed each other's company. I often flew pilot for Major Klette when weather was a problem, since he had high regard for my flying skills. He always co-piloted for me on missions, and we lived together in the Command Pilot House.

As I approached, he smiled, inquired about my flight, and asked, "Brownie, how would you like to go to London with me tomorrow? We have an invitation for cocktails and dinner; should be a great lot of fun." I replied, "Fine."

The next day we caught the early train from Royston and arrived in London several hours later. Since we were early, we dropped by *Wide Wing,* codename for USSTAF.

Later after lunch, we called at the country home of Mrs. Anthony Drexel Biddle, Jr. for cocktails and dinner. There were the three of us, for the Ambassador was on the Continent on business. We enjoyed the cocktails, and found Mrs. Biddle a charming woman, a skilled conversationalist. She was the complete mistress of the occasion with control, ease, composure and a wide versatility of topics seemingly at her fingertips. It was one of the nicest afternoons and evenings I can remember in England as our invitation progressed to dinner, which maintained the excellence.

Part of the household was a pitch-black Newfoundland dog by name of *Chan*. For the afternoon and evening I was a "Newfoundland" friend.

It was all wonderful; I shall never forget the hospitality extended by Mrs. Biddle.

We stayed that night at the city apartment quarters of a relative of the Queen of England. The luxurious accommodations were something that I have seldom seen, before or since. We returned the following day to Bassingbourn with another new experience added to our rapidly filling memories.

Nearing the End

Never in all our versatile experiences had we anticipated the adverse flying weather we found in these winter months in England. It was December and the fogs were impenetrable. Whiteness closed about the countryside as a vast heavy blanket. The winds were wet and penetrating, as moisture seemed to pierce the heaviest of materials, chilling the innermost bones. Rain poured from blackened skies, as lightning and thunder rivaled and surpassed the worst of man-made devices.

Combat missions were now less frequent and employed blind-bombing devices, *Mickey-Sets,* as well as the British *George-How,* or "G-H" equipment. On the 29th of November 1944, we bombed a rail yard at Misburg, Germany, with no outstanding incidents. On the 9th of December 1944, we attacked an installation at Stuttgart, Germany, with light losses. Then on the 18th of December 1944, we covered the troops with an attack at Luxemburg, Germany. All these missions were routine. The most difficult task was flying the weather and navigation.

My combat tour was winding toward a close with 28 accredited missions. I now spent considerable effort training a new *Lead* Pilot to assume Lead responsibilities. I was the only one left of all our **experienced** Lead Pilots, and the missions were wearing on my mental attitude. Sleep was now becoming more difficult. I found that I welcomed 4-5 hours sleep during the night and "*sweated*" other pilots' missions as though they were my own.

Our nervous systems had been heavily taxed, and I was ready for relief. I had not been allowed to take a rest at one of the many recuperation centers called *Flak Homes* that were merely accommodations away from the war-torn areas. There, for a period of ten days to two weeks you enjoyed the comforts of irresponsibility and complete rest from war and flying.

I was feeling the strain of nine months of sustained combat flying and had my sights elevated to the long trip home.

Stars and Stripes

The daily newspaper of the U.S. Armed Forces in England was the London Edition of Stars and Stripes. It was published in 4 pages and featured compact news items about the conduct of the War and various other areas of broad interest. The problem of secrecy plagued reporting War details, but this was understood. The military provided public releases that kept some continuity to the progress of the War. The general interest items came from the established news agencies.

It might be interesting for some to glance at a few headlines in a typical Stars and Stripes newspaper. The following news items appeared in the Stars and Stripes in late 1944:

Wednesday, December 27, 1944

- *700 Heavies strike at airdromes in the Frankfurt area (12/23)*
- *Nazis 4 mi. from Meuse – 50 miles into Belgium*
- *Nazi chutists hunt U.S. Chiefs with acid*
- *Leyte Battle over – M'Arthur*
- *Glenn Miller missing on hop from U.K. to Paris*
- *Stan Musial cops batting honors*
- *Trojans are strong favorite over Rose Bowl bound Vols*

- *Army heads may roll in wake of Nazi push*
- *House group to probe "news blackout" to troops*
- *Paris combed for Nazi spies – 30 arrested*

Thursday, December 28, 1944

- *600 Heavies hit again at rails (12/24)*
- *First enemy bombs in month hit Paris*
- *Marlene Dietrich out of films for duration*
- *Americans retake 2 towns at western extreme of Salient*
- *Since 12/17 start of German Drive Tactical Air Force claims to have destroyed 439 planes*
- *Report – "some German armor being abandoned for lack of fuel!" ***
- *Report – "Germans have been forced on defensive, with losses of armor from destruction and lack of fuel being so great that they had to throw in infantry in place of tanks." ***

The *Stars and Stripes* was popular, since it diverted attention away from personal war activities. It stimulated thoughts on what was happening elsewhere.

Note the likely impact of the low level destructive attack on the Merseburg Refinery Complex visibly starting to affect the War's progress.

Christmas in Combat

If you remember well, you will recall the black headlines that ushered in another Christmas at war in 1944. The essence of the news items was brief – the Germans had scored an amazing comeback in the fighting in eastern France. Whether by chance, fate, or brilliant meteorological guessing, the Germans counter-attacked our Armies at a weak point near Ardennes, France. What transpired is committed to World War II history, but the determinant factor of the German success was weather. In simultaneous coordination, the counter-attack was assisted by heavy fogs and the backwash of a frontal system that had stagnated over the Atlantic and over Central Germany. So, for several days the Allied Air Forces were grounded while Mr. Hitler's armies made a concerted *Pincer Drive (a military maneuver)* directed at Paris, France and Brussels, Belgium.

On the 24th of December 1944, we bombed a supply concentration point at Merzhauser, Germany, with no losses and light damage. We were unable to land at our own Base on our return due to a low persistent fog that blanketed Bassingborne. Other units were directed, as we were, to land at an alternate Base near the English Coast. A recapitulation of the Force at this Base revealed that over 160 *Flying Fortresses* were lined up on the runways practically *wing-to-wing*. This was the only practical and expeditious method possible under the circumstances. I was in command of 36 aircraft, and we were instructed to take precautions and await further orders.

Had the Germans known the circumstances, a dozen well-placed bombs could have reduced the equipment of three complete Groups to rubble, since the position and disposition of our aircraft was an auspicious one. We approached the problem as best we could—detailing partial crews to "stand by", to "man-the-guns" on the aircraft should any enemy intruder aircraft make an attack. In the meantime, we were briefed on the new problem that had arisen and awaited orders from higher headquarters. Our problem was this: we were sorely needed to support the troops on the front, but weather was expected which would immobilize the whole 8th Air Force and the 9th Air Force in England. If possible, we were to take our aircraft to the Continent and continue operations from new advance Bases of the 9th Air Force until such time, weather permitting, we could be released to return to England. We were to supply our own food and blankets, the aircraft would be our quarters, and bombs, gasoline, and ammunition would be supplied on the Continent.

In compliance with anticipated "Orders", our aircraft was loaded with a ten-day supply of rations for ten men. Blankets were then issued and we set ourselves for new "Orders".

At 2400 hours, or midnight, we were still awaiting "Orders", but the TWX was ominously silent. Crews were ordered to the planes to get sleep, since most had not slept for over 24 hours.

We waited in Operations for news. At last, at 0300 hours the TWX began, and "Orders" specifically verified our previous briefing. The operation was to "take place". An odd situation was beginning to develop—a heavy frost, almost like snow, began to form on the trees, the bushes, the buildings, and worst of all the aircraft.

The crews were summoned for briefing, and the mission was explained in detail to each formation. With no food for over 30 hours we returned to our B-17G's for another mission, but this time we were scheduled to land in France.

As we left the briefing, a transformation had occurred. As if by magic, icy white frost lay as snow over everything. The runways were obscured, and the once silver gleaming

Flying Fortresses were now white, encrusted with frost and ice, like ghost ships. The ice and frost on the windshields were so thick we were forced to use metal to scrape away the ice formation.

We were too late! The mission was impossible! Even as we vainly tried to make it work, as engines were "turned-over", the mission was "called off". After 33 hours of sleepless effort, sweat, and exhausting labor in freezing circumstances, it was all in vain. We returned tired and cold to await new "Orders".

It was Christmas Day. We were a tired and hungry aircrew on a strange Base and our immediate future still pending. We returned by lorry to our Base later that day to enjoy a hot Christmas Day dinner of turkey *with the trimmings*. Although we were exhausted, it was a wonderful Christmas Day and time for thanksgiving. It takes little perspective to conjure what might have been.

The Last One

A week later, on the 31st of December 1944, we entered the briefing room for the last time – this was my 30th combat mission. Weather was bad, but with luck and effort we could assist our troops at the front. Our target was Bitberg, Germany, and our aiming point was a troop concentration. Bombing was to be done *blind* with our special equipment. The mission was very successful and, otherwise, without incident, although I lost an engine due to mechanical failure. We returned to Bassingbourn and "touched-down" on the runway for the last time in England. This was the last time I handled the controls of a B-17 *Flying Fortress*.

My tour of combat duty was complete.

The future envisioned rest and, most of all, a one-way ticket to the good old United States——to milk shakes, to girls who spoke the American way, to football games, to a place where beer is beer and not lager, to the place we all loved dearly,

HOME.

Return

Following completion of air combat in the European Theater of Operation (ETO), I returned to the United States in early 1945 aboard the former luxury liner, USS Uruguay, which had been converted to a hospital ship. It was heart-breaking to see the broken and maimed bodies of young men injured primarily during the invasion of Western Europe. Each able Officer was assigned several wards to help the medical personnel. By and large, our assignments related to morale and personnel attention.

Infantry and tank personnel generally occupied my wards. More often than not, they enjoyed stories about flying and flying incidents.

For instance, one of stories was about a crash-landing I made after a mission to the Telemunde rocket laboratories. My B-17G had severe battle damage. I had lost hydraulics and, therefore, had no brakes, # 2 engine had a small fire, and only one landing gear would release to a landing and "lock" position. It was clear I had a problem! As I "belly-landed" the B-17G, I veered off the runway and finally stopped on top of an auxiliary bomb-storage dump. The #2 engine was still smoking, but no fire.

The aircrew exited the B-17G as quickly as they could. Since one of the B-17G engines was smoking, no one "offered" "to save us" until we had "cleared" the bomb dump and were several hundred yards from the bomb dump. The "savers" all stopped and kept waving to us "to hurry"! What a crash crew, they were!

The injured had me tell this story, and others, with comments, over and over again. (Incidentally, the bomb dump was relocated after this incident.)

Stories like this caused conversation—<u>everyone</u> had a story!

We returned in an escorted convoy and the slow convoy speed accentuated the debilitating and nauseous effects of the heavy, rolling winter seas of the North Atlantic Ocean. This anxious transit seemed to take *"forever and a day"*! We finally arrived in New York where I was detained at Fort Kilmer for debriefing and processing.

I returned to my home in Southern California on furlough in early 1945.

Telegrams

In civilian life during World War II, the family receipt of a telegram from the War Department is an indelible memory. Usually, the telegram explicitly announced in part that "We regret to inform you that your son was killed in action."

When I completed my 30th mission and received "Orders" to return to the USA, the War was still active. The blackout of information was still in effect. It was a period of silence until I arrived safely in the USA.

I made it an important priority to write my family bi-weekly. Needless to say, my letters stopped. It was a silence period of over a month. Upon my arrival in New York City, I exuberantly sent a telegram to my father's office in Placentia, California, a small town where everybody knew everybody. This was, in fact, a thoughtful, but thoughtless idea considering the circumstances of the silence period and the feared telegram syndrome of those times.

My father was advised that a telegram had been received and was in the process of being delivered. His secretary, Gladys Jennings, and his assistant, Joe Cline, with several others in his office staff gathered in his office to offer solace when the telegram arrived and was opened. It was a period of total anguish for all of them.

His recollection of the 30 minute wait for the delivery of the telegram and the thoughts that coursed through his mind were heart wrenching.

The anguish turned to exhilaration after reading the message that I had safely returned to the United States.

When he shared his experience with others, he always concluded, "I died for 30 minutes"!

Reassignment

After my "leave", I was reassigned in February, 1945 to a fighter operational training unit (OTU) at Greenwood, Mississippi AAFB. I completed training in P-51's, P-47's, and P-38's and waited for assignment to an Operational Squadron.

Because of my technical experience prior to military service, I was temporarily assigned to flight-test modified new fighters or to deliver modified or new fighter models to test sites. It was during a flight-test of a new rocket-firing P-38L that my appendix "ruptured" during the high performance flight test.

I was immediately hospitalized upon landing and survived complicated surgery. While recovering from surgery, I wrote notes and details and experiences of each mission of my USAF air combat in the European Theater of Operations (ETO). In February 1946, I used this data to produce a narrative of a tour of combat duty in B-17's.

Note: Capt. Ray M Brown was recalled for fighter air-combat service in Korea on October 23, 1951. His service was brief and he returned to civilian activities.

Reflections

World War II was a magnificent effort manned by very young men in their early twenties with huge responsibilities on their shoulders. The established military provided disciplines necessary for the conduct of the deadly conflict. The air war in World War II was carried out, however, by non-professionals executing these military stratagems.

Another war of the same size and international consequence as World War II is unlikely in the foreseeable future. It is a certainty that there will be future wars that complicate our present lives and freedoms. A major difference will be the loss of life and property in our homeland, this disturbing thought will stress the democratic freedoms that grace our present lives.

Future wars may extend for years without a clear "win or loss" decision, although the problems of the conflict may be partially solved. Many of these conflicts may be in underdeveloped countries with rogue leaders who have a misunderstood dislike or hate of democratic nations. Some of these conflicts may be carried out under the guise of religious "rights". The future will be plagued with the term, "Terrorist", which will be a catchall term for unlawful conduct. It is unlikely that the terrorist trend will end quickly, or ever. In fact, it may only be lessened, since zealots seem to have existed throughout our history, and they are difficult to defeat with lawful means. The main threats will clearly be small countries that are populated by dedicated extreme religious groups with economically poor living conditions. Their leaders will exhibit political and economic interests that feature gain of power, riches, land and recognition.

Technological developments in weaponry will complicate super-power execution of military stratagems, since small groups of zealots can acquire and use novel killing and destruction devices. The threat of biological and chemical weapons will cloud our future forever. While international organizations may intercede in conflicting causes in the future, major powers will not surrender to the conclusions and decisions of these organizations for years to come. The present century will tax the ingenuity of all free peoples to acquire and maintain security.

The threat of wars of mass destruction between super-powers will diminish, but it is likely that the possibility will play a part in national military planning. Super-powers will be driven to stratagems for defense capability.

Forecasting new weaponry for future conflicts involves improving present arms and ordnance, plus the likely addition of new equipment. Adding new equipment to the military inventory is slow, but demands for new military stratagems will quicken the pace of acceptance of new weapons and equipments. Available technology for the early 2000's will be utilized for the most part. It will be the basis for new weaponry for, at least, the first half of the 21st Century. There will be needs for new military organizations and new defense measures in which costs will be a major issue. Tradition of present Forces will oppose change, but change will happen. Redefinition of democratic freedoms and law and order will also be a major issue infiltrating our lives. The 21st century will be a historical era, and our lives will change dramatically.

The perplexing combination of conduct of wars and international political concurrence will aggravate all free people.

The pleasant thought is that free countries will prevail in the face of change.

Summary

It taxes one's wild imagination to think of the significant responsibilities very young American men and woman carried in World War II. As America exits the 20th Century, perhaps it's time to reflect with pride on the performance of these very young people who performed under immense pressure and great personal risk. The stakes were high—failure often meant death!

I left civilian life and entered the Army Air force Program in December of 1942. I was 24 years old, and opted to be a pilot.

The defeat of the German Nazi Forces was yet to be determined and the Luftwaffe was still an elite and formidable obstacle. German industry was heavily defended by anti-aircraft (flak) complexes that formed a wall of steel to penetrate.

Scarcely 18 months from a "behind a desk" civilian job, I was piloting a B-17G Heavy Bomber from Bassingbourn, England, the Base of the 91st Bomb Group. The 91st Bomb Group had been assigned the Lead Command of over 1000 Bombers on a deep penetration into a German industrial complex. I was 26 years old and Lead Command Pilot.

The task was to assemble 1000 B-17 aircraft, carrying tons of high explosives, into an efficient armada over England and, once formed, to lead the entire Air Force to destroy assigned targets in Germany. The outcome of World War II depended heavily on execution of these destructive tasks, day after day.

Consider the consequences of quickly "assembling" 1000 aircraft safely in a small air space over England without collision and disaster. A critical collision meant tons of high explosive falling on British cities with immense collateral damage and fires from the fuel load. Inefficient assembly meant loss of fuel capacity to reach and return from a target. In the European Theater of Operations (ETO), mission return over the last 30 miles was the English Channel, and insufficient fuel meant "ditching" the B-17 in the English Channel with the consequent danger of loss of life. This "assembly" procedure happened day-after-day in 1944—it was a part of "what we were supposed to do"!

The entire mission required instant decisions that were often "circumstance" and "unplanned". Enroute to a target, the Luftwaffe attacked Bombers with various stratagems. Bomber "close formation" meant increased protective firepower. "Changes in route" had to be carefully executed to hold the formations together, yet "changes in route" were necessary to avoid concentrations of anti-aircraft fire. "Target approach" required Bombers "in trail" to provide effective bomb patterns which meant that after "bombs away" the formations had to be reassembled quickly for protective reasons—the Luftwaffe was waiting!

The problems of reforming the armada as the mission returned was always further complicated by "battle damage" and the inability of some Bombers to hold formation well. Positioning the formation and vectoring American fighters to damaged bombers to provide protection was demanding on both fighters and the Group Commanders.

As the mission started, so it ended. The surviving bombers of the 1000 that initiated the mission returned en-masse to various Bases with the potential of collision and high danger. Again, the surviving 800-900 Bombers in the armada were "milling around England" to "touch-down" at a specific Base, and it had to be as orderly as possible. Imagine the problem!

Once in the returning "landing pattern", the "battle-damaged" Bombers and those with injured aircrew had first opportunity to land, so, again 30-40 Bombers (of the initial

54 Bombers) that formed a "returning" Bomb Group circumnavigated the Base while the unfortunate "touched-down". There were many Bases to accommodate 1000 Bombers, so the task was replicated in many nearby areas. This, also, was a "day-after-day" task.

The apparent excellence of these complicated and dangerous maneuvers is almost unimaginable. The necessary decisions and actions involved 10,000 young persons (1000 air crews) who were mostly under 26 years old. Many did not survive and families were disrupted, which is an American sadness!

I am the sole survivor of my Lead Aircrew—8 died in air combat.

It taxes the mind to think of the responsive performance and the "life and death" consequence of the many decisions made by these very young persons in the 20th Century. There are many "unsung" heroes who asked for very little. Perhaps, this is part of the patriotism that is America.

In the final analysis I find a warm pride in being a part of this generation and a Veteran.

Captain Ray M. Brown

About the Author

The Author, Ray M. Brown, was born in Fresno, California and now resides in West Bloomfield, Michigan. He graduated from Stanford University where he specialized in medicine and engineering. He added management skills to his background by participating in graduate business school executive sessions at Harvard University and Michigan State University.

During his undergraduate years he was a world-class athlete in track and field. His professional experience was largely in commercial and military research and development of advanced technology. He was employed as a Senior Scientist with Rockwell International and later organized his own consulting firm, specializing in the new technologies of the 2000's.

He was a technical advisor to the President of the United States, Mr. Nixon, on policies related to exporting important high technology.

He was distinguished in his flying and command skills in combat during World War II in the European Theater of Operation (ETO) receiving three Distinguished Flying Crosses and five Air Medals. He was particularly noted for his Lead Pilot skills where he commanded large B-17 Bomber formations often exceeding 1000 aircraft.

At 87 years of age, he is now retired, in good health, and enjoys the company of his twin daughters and wife of 54 years.

Printed in the United States
by Baker & Taylor Publisher Services